Critters
of Arizona
Pocket Guide to Animals in Your State

ALEX
TROUTMAN
produced in cooperation with
Wildlife Forever

PUBLICATIONS
adventure
an imprint of AdventureKEEN

About Wildlife Forever

Wildlife Forever works to conserve America's outdoor heritage through conservation education, preservation of habitat, and scientific management of fish and wildlife. Wildlife Forever is a 501c3 nonprofit organization dedicated to restoring habitat and teaching the next generation about conservation. Become a member and learn more about innovative programs like the Art of Conservation®, The Fish and Songbird Art Contests®, Clean Drain Dry Initiative™, and Prairie City USA®. For more information, visit wildlifeforever.org.

Thank you to Ann McCarthy, the original creator of the Critters series, for her dedication to wildlife conservation and to environmental education. Ann dedicates her work to her daughters, Megan and Katharine Anderson.

Front cover photos by **Kanyshev Andrey/shutterstock.com:** white-nosed coati, **CuorerouC/shutterstock.com:** Harris's hawk, **Vaclav Sebek/shutterstock.com:** Gila monster
Back cover photo by **Dennis W Donohue/Shutterstock.com:** collared peccary

Edited by Brett Ortler and Jenna Barron
Cover and book design by Jonathan Norberg
Proofreader: Emily Beaumont

10 9 8 7 6 5 4 3 2 1

Critters of Arizona
First Edition 2002, Second Edition 2024
Copyright © 2002 by Wildlife Forever, Copyright © 2024 by Alex Troutman
The first edition (2002) of this book was produced by Wildlife Forever.
AdventureKEEN is grateful for its continued partnership and advocacy
on behalf of the natural world.

Published by Adventure Publications
An imprint of AdventureKEEN
310 Garfield Street South, Cambridge, Minnesota 55008
(800) 678-7006
www.adventurepublications.net
All rights reserved
Printed in China
Cataloging-in-Publication data is available from the Library of Congress
ISBN 978-1-64755-462-0 (pbk.); 978-1-64755-463-7 (ebook)

Acknowledgments

I want to thank everyone who believed in and supported me over the years—a host of friends, family, and teachers. I want to especially thank my mom and my siblings Van, Bre, and TJ.

Dedication

I dedicate this book to my brother Van:
May you continue to enjoy the birds and wildlife in heaven.

This book is for all the kids who have a passion for nature and the outdoors, especially ones who identify as Black, Brown, Indigenous, and People of Color. May this be an encouragement to never give up. And if you have a dream and passion for something, pursue it relentlessly. I also hope to set an example that you can be successful as your full, authentic self!

Lastly, I dedicate this book to all those with ADHD and dyslexia, as well as all other members of the neurodivergent community. While our quirks make things more challenging, our goals are not impossible to reach; sometimes it takes a little more time and help, but we, too, can succeed!

Contents

Reptiles and Amphibians

Introduction

My passion for nature started when I was young. I was always amazed by the sunlit fiery glow of the red-tailed hawks as they soared overhead when I went fishing with my family. The red-tailed hawk was my spark bird—the bird that captures your attention and gets you into birding. Through my many encounters with red-tailed hawks, and other species like garter snakes and coyotes, I found a passion for nature and the environment. Stumbling across conservationists like Steve Irwin, Jeff Corwin, and Jack Hanna introduced me to the field of Wildlife Biology as a career and gave birth to a dream that I was able to accomplish and live out: serving as a Fish and Wildlife Biologist for governmental agencies, as well as in the private sector.

My childhood dream was driven by a desire to learn more about the different types of ecosystems and the animals that call our wild places home. Books and field guides like this one whet my thirst for knowledge. Even before I could fully understand the words on the pages, I was drawn to books and flashcards that had animals on them. I could soon identify every animal I was shown and tell a fact about it. I hope that this edition of *Critters of Arizona* can be the fuel that sustains your passion for not only learning about wildlife, but also for caring for the environment and making sure that all are welcome in the outdoors. For others, may this book be the spark that ignites a flame for wildlife preservation and environmental stewardship. I hope that this book inspires children from lower socioeconomic and minority backgrounds to pursue their dreams to the fullest and be unapologetically themselves.

By profession, I'm a Fish and Wildlife Biologist, and I'm a nature enthusiast through and through. My love for nature includes making sure that everyone has an equal opportunity to enjoy the outdoors in their own way. So, as you use this book, I encourage you to be intentional in inviting others to appreciate nature with you. Enjoy your discoveries and stay curious!

–Alex Troutman

Arizona: The Grand Canyon State

Arizona is known for its beautiful desert landscapes, including the Grand Canyon, Petrified Forest, and the Painted Desert. But the state is much more diverse than many people think, with mountains, forests, grasslands, and even moist areas around the Colorado River floodplains. Many Indigenous tribes, such as the Navajo, Apache, and Hopi, have lived on the land for thousands of years, well before the Spanish arrived in the 1530s. The state, along with California, Utah, Nevada, and New Mexico, was a part of Mexico until the end of the Mexican–American War, which in 1848 was won by the United States. It became a state in 1912.

In fact, at its northeast corner, there is a place where you can be in Arizona, Utah, Colorado, and New Mexico all at once! In the northwest part of the state is its most famous landmark (and the reason for its nickname): the Grand Canyon. It was carved over time by the Colorado River through a process called erosion; its deepest point is 6,000 feet, but it is still home to many animals such as pronghorns and hawks. In northeastern Arizona is the Petrified Forest National Park, which preserves the trees and animals that were in the area 200 million years ago. The Sonoran Desert takes up most of the southern part of the state and is home to many wild reptiles not seen anywhere else in the US.

These environments are home to many animals, including 144 species of mammals, 570 species of birds, and 151 species of reptiles and amphibians, not to mention fish, countless insects and spiders, plants, and more. This is your guide to the animals, birds, reptiles, and amphibians that call Arizona home.

Some of Arizona's most iconic plants, animals, and other natural resources are now officially recognized as state symbols. Get to know them below and see if you can spot them all! You'll probably encounter the state nickname and motto, so I've included them here too.

State Bird:
cactus wren

State Gem:
turquoise

State Tree:
palo verde

State Flower:
white blossom of the saguaro

State Fish:
Apache trout

State Amphibian:
Arizona tree frog

State Reptile:
ridge-nosed rattlesnake

State Mammal:
ringtail

State Nickname:
The Grand Canyon State

State Butterfly:
two-tailed swallowtail

State Motto:
Ditat Deus
("God enriches")

How to Use This Guide

This book is your introduction to some of the wonderful critters found in Arizona; it includes 23 mammals, 23 birds, and 18 reptiles and amphibians. It includes some animals you probably already know, such as striped skunks and bald eagles, but others you may not know about, such as spadefoot toads or phainopeplas. I've selected the species in this book because they are widespread (northern raccoon, page 48), abundant (red-winged blackbird, page 94), or well-known but best observed from a safe distance (sidewinder rattlesnake, page 122).

The book is organized by types of animals: mammals, birds, and reptiles and amphibians. Within each section, the animals are in alphabetical order. If you'd like to look for a critter quickly, turn to the checklist (page 140), which you can also use to keep track of how many animals you've seen! For each species, you'll see a photo of the animal, along with neat facts and information on the animal's habitat, diet, its predators, how it raises its young, and more.

Safety Note

Nature can be unpredictable, so don't go outdoors alone, and always tell an adult when you're going outside. All wild animals should be treated with respect. If you see one—big or small—don't get close to it or attempt to touch or feed it. Instead, keep your distance and enjoy spotting it. If you can, snap some pictures with a camera or make a quick drawing using a sketchbook. If the animal is getting too close, is acting strangely, or seems sick or injured, tell an adult right away, as it might have rabies, a disease that can affect mammals. The good news is there's a rabies vaccine, so it's important to visit a doctor right away if you get bit or scratched by a wild animal.

Notes About Icons

Each species page includes basic information about an animal, from what it eats to how it survives the winter. The book also includes information that's neat to know; in the mammals section, each page includes a simple track illustration of the animal, with approximate track size included. And along the bottom, there is an example track pattern for the mammal, with the exception for those that primarily glide or fly (flying squirrels and bats).

On the left-hand page for each mammal, a rough-size illustration is included that shows how big the animal is when compared to a basketball.

Also on the left-hand page, there are icons that tell you when each animal is most active: nocturnal (at night), diurnal (during the day), or crepuscular (at dawn/dusk), so you know when to look. If an animal has a "zzz" icon, it hibernates during the winter. Some animals hibernate every winter, and their internal processes (breathing and heartbeat) slow down almost entirely. Other animals only partially hibernate, but this still helps them save energy and survive through the coldest part of the year.

nocturnal
(active at night)

diurnal
(active during day)

crepuscular
(most active at
dawn and dusk)

hibernates/deep sleeper
(dormant during winter)

ground nest

cup nest

platform nest

cavity nest

migrates

On the left-hand side of each bird page, the nest for the species is shown, along with information on whether or not the bird migrates; on the right-hand side, there's information on where it goes.

Did you know?

Badgers are solitary animals, but they will sometimes hunt with coyotes in a team. A coyote will chase prey into the badger's den, and the badger will chase or dig out the prey that coyotes like. The badger's den has one entrance with a pile of dirt next to it. When a badger is threatened, it will back into its burrow and show its teeth.

Size Comparison   Most Active   Track Size   Hibernates

   2¾"

American Badger

Taxidea taxus

Size: 2–3 feet long; weighs 8–25 pounds

Habitat: Savannas, grasslands, and meadows

Range: Can be found throughout the Midwest and westward through the Great Plains to the western coast of the United States and southward into Mexico. They are found throughout the state of Arizona.

Food: Carnivores; they eat pocket gophers, moles, ground squirrels, and other rodents. They will also eat dead animals (or carrion), fish, reptiles, and a few types of birds, especially ground-nesting birds.

Den: Badgers are fossorial (a digging animal that spends a lot of time underground); they build many dens or burrows throughout their range. Most dens are used to store food, but badgers also use dens to sleep in and raise their young. Dens can be over 10 feet deep and 4 feet wide.

Young: Cubs are born, with eyes closed, usually in April or May in litters of 2–3. Extensive care is provided by the mom for up to 3 months. After another 2–3 months, the young will gain their independence.

Predators: Bears, bobcats, mountain lions, coyotes, golden eagles, and humans

Tracks: The front tracks are 2¾ inches long and 2 inches wide.

The American badger is a short, bulky mammal with grayish-to-dirty-red fur. Badgers have a distinctive face with a series of cream-and-white stripes offset by a black background.

Did you know?

The hog-nosed skunk is the largest skunk in North America and one of the largest in the world! It gets its name from its slightly upturned nose. They are also sometimes called rooter skunks because of the way they overturn the ground and rocks while foraging (or searching) for food.

Size Comparison   Most Active   Track Size

2½"

American Hog-nosed Skunk

Conepatus leuconotus

Size: 41 inches long (with tail); weighs 2–3 pounds

Habitat: Deserts, forested areas, and rocky outcrops

Range: They can be found from Central America up into southwestern United States such as Nevada, Arizona, New Mexico, Oklahoma, Texas, and Colorado. In Arizona, they are found in the southeastern area of the state.

Food: They are omnivores that mainly feed on insects, carrion (dead animals), fruits, mammals, reptiles, and berries.

Den: They dig burrows to rest during the day, as well as for birthing and raising young.

Young: 1–5 young are born between April and May. Young will reach independence by the following August.

Predators: Coyotes, red wolves, American badgers, mountain lions, and raptors like eagles and owls

Tracks: Both sets of feet have five toes with claw marks and pads. Front claws are longer than hind claws. Hind foot is 2½ inches long.

The American hog-nosed skunk has a broad white stripe that runs from the head to the tail. The tail is long and all white. They have a long, furless, and somewhat upturned nose. Their large forelimbs with big claws help them dig up insects.

Did you know?

The Arizona myotis was once thought to be a subspecies of the little brown bat; however, in 2002, it was reclassified as its own species. Also called the southwestern little brown bat, the Arizona myotis can echolocate at a rate of 200 calls per second when hunting prey. Nursing females can eat more than their body weight in insects each night.

Size Comparison   Most Active

Arizona Myotis

Myotis occultus

Size: 3¼–3½ inches long; wingspan of 9½–9¾ inches; weighs ¼ ounce

Habitat: Caves, mines, and other human structures like bridges and buildings; forests; rocky areas; and wetlands

Range: They can be found in the western parts of the United States from southeastern California, Arizona, New Mexico, and Texas; their range extends into central Mexico. In Arizona, they can be found in central and eastern parts of the state.

Food: They are carnivores that feed on insects.

Den: Roost sites are usually near water and oftentimes in caves. Human structures like bridges, abandoned buildings, and mines are also used as roost sites. Bats nest in colonies from as few as 40 bats to more than 2,000.

Young: 1–2 pups are born after a 50–60-day pregnancy. They wean around 3 weeks and are reproductively mature within a year for females and 2 years for males.

Predators: Raccoons, hawks, owls, snakes, and mice

Tracks: Though they are rarely on the ground to leave a track, it would show one thumbprint on the front and the hind footprint.

The Arizona myotis is a small mammal with brown, glossy fur and dark-brown-to-black ears, nose, and wings. The back is darker than the stomach area and face.

Did you know?

The largest wild sheep in North America is the bighorn sheep. Their horns can be over 3 feet long, as thick as 1 foot, and can weigh over 20 pounds. Bighorn sheep are agile, able to run over 30 miles per hour and jump over 19 feet from one ledge to another.

Size Comparison   Most Active   Track Size

2½—3½"

18

Bighorn Sheep

Ovis canadensis

Size: 5–6 feet long; weighs 125–200 pounds or more

Habitat: Alpine meadows; grassy mountain slopes; and foothill country close to rugged, rocky cliffs and bluffs

Range: In Arizona, they can be found throughout the western and southern half of the state with a range that extends eastward. They can also be found in the Rocky Mountains, southern California, Utah, New Mexico, and Texas.

Food: Grasses, clovers, sedges, and flowers

Den: No den

Young: One lamb is born around 150–180 days after breeding. Young are precocial, meaning they are able to walk and stand a few minutes to hours after birth. By months 4–6, lambs are weaned. During the first year of life, they learn their home territory. Males will leave their mom at 2–4 years old to join a male group, and females will usually stay with their mom for life.

Predators: Wolves, coyotes, golden eagles, bears, and mountain lions

Tracks: Front and hind tracks are 2½–3½ inches long and 1¾–2½ inches wide.

Both male and female bighorn sheep have light-to-dark-brown fur; they sometimes have a grayish hue. Their muzzle, backs of legs, and rump are white. The males (rams) have large, circular horns that frame their face. Females (ewes, pronounced like "yous") have shorter horns that are not as circular. Young (lambs) are grayish with a blackish-brown tail.

Did you know?

Female bears weigh between 90 and 300 pounds and are smaller than the average adult human male in the US. But don't let their small size fool you; with a bite force around 800 pounds per square inch (PSI) and swiping force of over 400 pounds, these bears are not to be taken lightly.

Size Comparison   Most Active   Track Size   Hibernates

  6–7"

Black Bear
Ursus americanus

Size: 5–6 feet long (nose to tail); weighs 90–600 pounds

Habitat: Forests, lowland areas, and swamps

Range: Black bears can be found in many parts of North America, from Alaska down through Canada and into Mexico. They can be found in the central-eastern portion of the state below the Grand Canyon.

Food: Berries, fish, seeded crops, small mammals, wild grapes, tree shoots, ants, bees, beavers, and even deer fawns

Den: Denning usually starts in December, with bears emerging in late March or April. Dens can be either dug (out of a hillside, for example) or constructed with materials such as leaves, grass, and moss.

Young: Two cubs are usually born at one time (a litter), often in January. Cubs are born without fur and blind, with pink skin. They weigh 8–16 ounces.

Predators: Humans and other bears. Sometimes, other carnivores, such as mountain lions, wolves, coyotes, or even bobcats, will prey on black bears. Cubs are especially vulnerable.

Tracks: Front print is usually 4–6 inches long and 3½–5 inches wide, with the hind foot being 6–7 inches long and 3½–5 inches wide. The feet have five toes.

Black bears are usually black in color, but they can be many different variations of black and brown. Some even have grayish, reddish, or blonde fur.

Did you know?
Black-footed ferrets are the only ferret species native to North America. A group of ferrets is called a business. Ferrets sleep over 20 hours a day. Their body is the same width from their neck down to their hips.

Size Comparison

Most Active

Track Size

1¾"

Black-footed Ferret

Mustela nigripes

Size: 16–24 inches long; weighs 2–3 pounds

Habitat: Grasslands, shrublands, and prairies

Range: At one time, they were found in 12 states across the US and portions of Mexico and Canada. Now, they are only found in isolated reintroduced populations in a few states, including Arizona, where they inhabit the central portion of the state.

Food: Carnivores that mainly eat prairie dogs, they also eat rodents and other small animals.

Den: Underground burrow; most of the time they use abandoned prairie dog burrows that are further excavated (dug out).

Young: 1–6 kits are born after a 35–45-day pregnancy. Kits will stay in the burrow for about 6 weeks (42 days) before coming out. Kits will separate by the fall of their birth year and become reproductively mature at 1 year old.

Predators: Owls, hawks, badgers, coyotes, and bobcats

Tracks: Tracks are around 1¾ inches long and 1 inch wide.

Black-footed ferrets have long, slender bodies and claws that are yellowish brown to black. They have a buffy-light-brown underside, with blackish feet and a dark mask around their widely spaced eyes. Their ears and tails sport a black tracing. They have a round face with a short muzzle and legs.

Did you know?

Black-tailed jackrabbits are hares, not rabbits. The difference is that rabbits are smaller and born without fur, while hares are larger and born with fur. Jackrabbits have powerful legs that allow them to reach speeds of over 30 miles per hour and leap more than 10 feet in length.

Size Comparison   Most Active   Track Size

2½—5½"

Black-tailed Jackrabbit

Lepus californicus

Size: 2 feet long; weighs 3–9 pounds

Habitat: Brushlands, desert scrublands, farmlands, prairies, and meadows

Range: They can be found in the western United States from southern Washington into California and as far east as Nebraska and Texas. They can be found throughout Arizona.

Food: Jackrabbits are herbivores that mainly eat plants like alfalfa and clover. In the fall and winter months, they will also eat woody vegetation.

Den: No den; bunnies are born in scratched-out, hollow depressions.

Young: Bunnies are born at around 40 days after pregnancy. They are born with hair and are active soon after birth. Young nurse for only a few days and reach reproductive maturity within their first year.

Predators: Coyotes, foxes, bobcats, badgers, and weasels

Tracks: Front feet are around 2–2½ inches long and 1¼–1¾ inches wide. Hind feet are 2½–5½ inches long and around 1½–2½ inches wide.

The black-tailed jackrabbit is a large, long-eared hare. It has dark, peppery-brown fur and black-tipped ears. The black-tailed jackrabbit has very long front and rear legs. It has a black stripe that runs down its back. Males and females look alike, but females are usually larger.

Did you know?

Even though they are called prairie dogs, they are not in the canine or dog family; they are actually rodents belonging to the squirrel family. The black-tailed is the most common of the prairie dog species. Prairie dogs use a variety of vocalizations to communicate. They will even "bark" to alert others to danger.

Size Comparison   Most Active   Track Size

1–2"

Black-tailed Prairie Dog

Cynomys ludovicianus

Size: 14–17 inches long; weighs 2–3 pounds

Habitat: Grassy plains and prairies

Range: They are found in the Great Plains east of the Rocky Mountains and into Mexico. In Arizona, they can be found in the southeastern corner of the state.

Food: Grasses, seeds, plants, and sometimes insects

Den: They live in multi-burrow colonies called "towns." Burrows can be 3–6 feet wide, sometimes as deep as 15 feet underground, and have several chambers. The nest chamber is usually lined with grass.

Young: One litter of 3–5 pups is born after 30–35 days of pregnancy. Pups are born hairless and blind. They open their eyes around 5 weeks and will start exploring outside the burrow around the same time. Both parents care for young and, once they are aboveground, any female producing milk will nurse them. They will leave the coterie (group of prairie dogs) at 1 year old.

Predators: Black-footed ferrets are their main predators; snakes, eagles, coyotes, hawks, falcons, and badgers.

Tracks: The front foot is 1–1½ inches long and hind foot is 1–2 inches long. Both sets are ⅞–1⅜ inches wide with claw marks at the end of each toe.

Prairie dogs come in various shades of brown and tan. They have small, thick bodies; rounded ears; a short tail; sharp teeth; and strong claws for digging. Their tail is black at the tip, hence their name.

Did you know?
Bobcats get their name from their short tail; a "bob" is a type of short haircut. They have the largest range of all wild cats in the United States. Bobcats can even hunt prey much larger than themselves; in fact, they can take down prey that is over four times their size, such as white-tailed deer!

Size Comparison   Most Active   Track Size

2"

Bobcat

Lynx rufus

Size: 27–48 inches head to tail; males weigh around 30 pounds, while females weigh 24 pounds or so.

Habitat: Dense forests, scrub areas (forests of low trees and bushes), swamps, and even some urban (city) areas

Range: They are widespread throughout the United States. Bobcats are found statewide in Arizona.

Food: Squirrels, birds, rabbits, white-tailed jackrabbits, and white-tailed deer fawns; occasionally even adult deer!

Den: Dense shrubs, caves, or even hollow trees; dens can be lined with leaves or moss.

Young: Bobcats usually breed in early winter through spring. Females give birth to a litter of 2–4 kittens. Bobcats become independent around 7–8 months, and they reach reproductive maturity at 1 year for females and at 2 years for males.

Predators: Occasionally coyotes; humans also hunt and trap bobcats for fur.

Tracks: Roughly 2 inches wide; both front and back paws have four toe pads and a carpal pad (a pad below the toe pads).

Bobcats have a white belly and a brown or pale-gray top with black spots. The tail usually has a black tip. They are mostly crepuscular (say it, cre-pus-cue-lar), which means they are most active in the dawn and twilight hours.

Did you know?

Collared peccaries are not pigs! In fact, they do not share any recent ancestors. One way to distinguish them is that collared peccaries' tails are stumped and not easily visible, while pigs' tails are long. Also, collared peccaries have a scent gland on the top of their rump, while pigs do not. They will use this gland to rub their scent on trees and rocks to mark territory.

Size Comparison   Most Active   Track Size

1¼"

Collared Peccary

Pecari tacaju

Size: 14–17 inches long; weighs 2–3 pounds

Habitat: Brush country, grasslands, woodlands, and semi-desert rocky canyons

Range: They can be found from southwestern Texas down into Central America and as far south as Argentina. In Arizona, they are found throughout the central and southeastern portions of the state.

Food: They feed on various cacti, fruits, other types of vegetation, insects, and sometimes snakes.

Den: They have no permanent nests or dens but lie down as a group in grassy areas.

Young: Usually 2 young are born per litter after a pregnancy of almost 5 months. Young are sometimes called "reds" because of the color of their hair. Males become reproductively mature at around 46–47 weeks and females at around 33–34 weeks.

Predators: Mountain lions, humans, coyotes, bobcats, and jaguars

Tracks: The front feet have four hoofed toes, and the hind feet have three, though only two toe prints are noticeable.

Collared peccaries look like small, hairy pigs, minus a tail. They have a white-to-cream-colored collar on top of a black coarse-coated body. The white collar is where they get their name. Females and males look the same. They have small eyes, large heads, and tusks on both the top and bottom jaws.

Did you know?

At one time, coyotes were only found in the central and western parts of the US, but now, with the help of humans (eliminating predators and clearing forests), they can be found throughout most of the country.

Size Comparison   Most Active   Track Size

2"

Coyote

Canis latrans

Size: 3–4 feet long; weighs 21–50 pounds

Habitat: Urban and suburban areas, woodlands, grasslands, and farm fields

Range: Coyotes can be found throughout Arizona. They are also found throughout the US and Mexico, the northern parts of Central America, and in southern Canada.

Food: A variety of prey, including rodents, birds, deer, and sometimes livestock

Den: Coyotes will dig their own dens but will often use old fox or badger dens or hollow logs.

Young: 5–7 pups, independent around 8–10 months

Predators: Bears and wolves; humans trap and kill for pelts and to "protect" livestock.

Tracks: Four toes and a carpal pad (the single pad below the toe pads) can be seen on all four feet.

Coyotes have brown, reddish-brown, or gray back fur with a lighter gray-to-white belly. They have a longer muzzle than other wild canines. They are active mostly during the night (nocturnal) but also during the twilight and dawn hours (crepuscular).

Did you know?

Shrews have glands that produce a musky odor that they use to signal when they are ready to mate and claim a territory. Like bats and dolphins, desert shrews use echolocation to find food.

Size Comparison   Most Active   Track Size

¼"

Desert Shrew

Notiosorex crawfordi

Size: 2–3 inches long; weighs 4½–8 grams

Habitat: Canyons, forests, woodlands, mountainous areas, shrublands, grasslands, deserts, and wetlands

Range: They are found from western Texas westward to the Pacific Coast, with ranges in Colorado, Oklahoma, New Mexico, Utah, Nevada, and Arkansas, as well as in central Mexico. In Arizona, they are found almost statewide.

Food: Carnivores, they feed on insects and small invertebrates.

Den: Built under logs, stumps, and rocks; lined with grass, leaves, and roots

Young: 5–7 young are born furless with eyes closed after about a month-long pregnancy. They are smaller than bees at birth and develop quickly. They are weaned in about a month and are considered independent. They reach reproductive maturity at around 2 months.

Predators: Snakes, hawks, and owls

Tracks: Both hind and front tracks are about ¼-inch long and wide. Both feet have five toes.

The desert shrew is a small mammal with a tubular or cylinder-shaped body. They have short limbs, small eyes, and rounded ears. Their fur is brown to dusky gray on the back and paler on the underside or belly area.

Did you know?

Elk are known to be the loudest of all cervids (deer family). Males produce a low-pitched bellow or roar, called a bugle. Bugling is a technique that involves both roaring and whistling at the same time. Elk use their bugle or bugling to attract mates or announce territories during the fall mating season. Their bugles can be heard over long distances.

Size Comparison   Most Active   Track Size

4½"

Elk

Cervus elaphus canadensis

Size: 5–8 feet tall; weighs 377–1,095 pounds

Habitat: Open woodlands, mountain areas, shrublands, coniferous swamps, and hardwood forests

Range: Found throughout the western US, portions of the Southeast, and in Canada. In Arizona, they are found in central and eastern parts of the state.

Food: Elk are herbivores that eat grasses; flowers; and leaves from trees like cedar, red maple, and basswood.

Den: No den; will lay in grass to rest. Mother elk will hide young calves in tall grasses.

Young: Calves are born after 240–265 days. At birth, calves weigh around 30 pounds and have spots through the first summer. Separation from mother's milk happens around the 60-day mark, but calves will continue to get care and protection from mom for around a year. They reach full maturity around 16 months, but males will usually wait to mate until they are older.

Predators: Mountain lions, Mexican gray wolves, and bears. Calves may fall victim to bobcats and coyotes.

Tracks: Front tracks of an adult are about 4¾ inches long and wide. Hind foot tracks are 4½ inches long and 3½ inches wide. Two toes are on both feet.

Elk come in different shades of browns and tans. In the summer and spring they are lighter brown to tan, while in the winter they are a deep dark brown; during both seasons, they have a cream or off-white rump. They sport a darker tone on the head, neck, belly, and legs.

Did you know?

While kangaroo rats are rodents, they are not actually rats.
Kangaroo rats get their name from their long feet and the
way they jump in a bipedal (moving on two limbs) motion
like kangaroos! They can jump over 9 feet in the air when scared.

Size Comparison   Most Active   Track Size

1¼–2"

38

Merriam's Kangaroo Rat

Dipodomys merriami

Size: 14 inches long (3½–5½-inch body, 5½–6½-inch tail; weighs 1½–1¾ ounces

Habitat: Shrublands, deserts, forests, woodlands, and scrub areas

Range: They can be found in the southwestern United States starting in California, then eastward into Nevada, New Mexico, Utah, Arizona, and Texas. They are also found in Mexico. In Arizona, they are found in the Sonoran Desert.

Food: Herbivores, they eat plants and seeds. They rarely drink water and instead get it from the plants they eat.

Den: February–May is when mating takes place; they use underground dens that they dig.

Young: After around a month of pregnancy, 4 kittens (young) are born. They will become independent within 25–33 days and reach maturity within 3 months.

Predators: Owls, snakes, bobcats, foxes, badgers, coyotes, and pet cats and dogs

Tracks: Hind feet have five toes with long claws (front tracks are rarely left due to hopping motion). Track size can be 1¼–2 inches. Hind feet tracks are usually seen side by side.

Merriam's kangaroo rats are small rodents with large hind feet; they have a long, tufted tail that aids in balance. They are brown to light tan on the back and pale to white on the front or belly area.

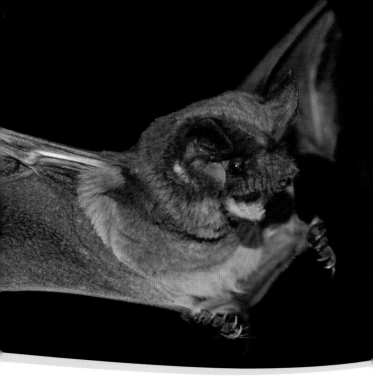

Did you know?

Mexican free-tailed bats are the fastest-known mammals on Earth, even faster than a cheetah at over 99 miles per hour (mph). A colony of Mexican free-tailed bats can consume over 250 tons of insects in a night; this makes them great at pest control for farmers. Sometimes they fly over 10,000 feet high. They get their name from the little section of tail that sticks out from their skin.

Size Comparison   Most Active

Mexican Free-tailed Bat

Tadarida brasiliensis

Size: 3–4 inches long; wingspan is 11–12 inches; weighs ¼–½ ounce

Habitat: Wetland areas, caves, suburban areas, urban areas, forests, and deserts

Range: They are found throughout most of the southern half of the US. They can be found throughout Arizona until the fall, when they migrate Mexico to overwinter.

Food: Carnivores; moths, beetles, flies, and dragonflies

Den: Roost sites are usually near water and in caves. Human structures like bridges, abandoned buildings, and mines are also used. Bats nest in colonies from as few as 40 bats to up to several thousand.

Young: One pup is born 11–12 weeks after mating. Pups roost in high areas where it is hot. Pups are raised by females. In about 4–7 weeks, they are independent. They can reproduce at around 9 months for females and 2 years for males.

Predators: Barn owls, red-tailed hawks, skunks, raccoons, and snakes

Tracks: Though they are rarely on the ground to leave a track, it would show one thumbprint from the forearm and a hind footprint.

The Mexican free-tailed bat is also known as the Brazilian free-tailed bat. Mexican free-tailed bats are medium-size bats. They are dark brown to clay-red in color. They have large ears with black tips, a short nose, and wrinkled lips. They have long, narrow wings and a small, exposed tail.

The Mexican free-tailed bat does not often leave tracks.

Did you know?

Mexican gray wolves are the smallest of the gray wolves that can be found in the United States. They can eat 20 pounds of meat in one sitting. The Mexican gray wolf is the most endangered species of wolf; at one time, there were only a few left in zoos. Now, through reintroduction of 11 wolves in Arizona, their population has increased, though they are still critically endangered.

Size Comparison   Most Active   Track Size

   3½—4"

Mexican Gray Wolf

Canis lupus baileyi

Size: 4½–5 feet long; weighs 59½–79¼ pounds

Habitat: Woodlands, grasslands, forests, scrublands, and mountainous forests

Range: At one time, they were widespread across much of the southwestern half of North America. Today, they are currently only found in southeastern Arizona, with some sightings in New Mexico, and they have been reintroduced into Mexico.

Food: Carnivores, they feed on ground squirrels, mice, and other small mammals, as well as elk and pronghorn deer.

Den: Burrowed-out hole, rock crevice, or hole under a tree stump or log

Young: 4–7 pups are born about 2 months after mating. They reach independence in 5 weeks and reproductive maturity in about 2 years.

Predators: Other wolves, humans, mountain lions, and black bears

Track: 3½–4 inches long and 3¼–3¾ inches wide

Mexican gray wolves are smaller than other wolves found in North America. They have a smaller and more narrow head. Their fur is a darker color with a yellowish-gray tint; their back and tail are darkened with black.

Did you know?

Mountain lions are the second-largest cat in the western part of the world. The largest is the jaguar. Mountain lions do not roar like other big cats, but rather they scream! They also make other sounds similar to pet cats, like hissing and purring. Mountain lions can jump as high as 18 feet off the ground into a tree.

Size Comparison   Most Active   Track Size

Mountain Lion

Puma concolor

Size: 6–8 feet long; weighs 100–154 pounds

Habitat: Grasslands, deserts, wetlands, shrublands, forests, swamps, and upland forests

Range: They can be seen from northern Canada to Argentina. They can be found throughout Arizona.

Food: Deer, wild boars, raccoons, birds, rabbits, mice, and occasionally livestock

Den: Will den in caves, rock piles and crevices, and thickets. Dens are usually lined with plants.

Young: 1–6 kittens are born with spots almost 100 days after mating. Weaning takes place around day 4, and the young kits will stay with their mom another year or two. Spots fade at around 6 months. Males reach reproductive maturity at around 3 years old and females around 2½ years, though they usually do not reproduce until they have a permanent home territory.

Predators: No natural predators, but they will sometimes get in territory disputes with other large carnivores.

Tracks: Front tracks are 3¼ inches long and wide. The back or hind tracks are 3 inches long and wide.

Mountain lion fur is golden tan to dusky brown on the back; its underside is a pale buff color with a white throat and chest area. They have a pink nose, black ear tips, and a smoky gray-black muzzle. The tip of their tail is black like their ears, and their eyes are brown. Their tail is long and makes up a third of their body length. Kittens have spots and smoky-blue eyes.

Did you know?

Mule deer get their name from their large ears that resemble those of mules. When they first emerge, a deer's antlers are covered in a special skin called velvet. Deer can run up to 40 miles per hour and can jump over 8 feet vertically (high) and over 15 feet horizontally (long). Mule deer and other deer species do not have teeth on the top of their mouth, just a hard palate.

Size Comparison   Most Active   Track Size

Mule Deer

Odocoileus hemionus

Size: 4–7 feet long; 3–3½ feet tall; weighs 200–260 pounds

Habitat: Forest edges, brushy fields, woody farmlands, prairies, deserts, and mountainous and rocky areas

Range: They are found from California to the Missouri River. In Arizona, they are common statewide.

Food: Fruits, grasses, trees, shrubs, nuts, and bark

Den: Deer do not den, but they will bed down in tall grasses and shrub areas.

Young: After a 200-day pregnancy, fawns (young) are born with spots and weigh around 5½ pounds. They lay in the same spot where they're born for about a week or so. They lose their spots and are weaned at around 2–2½ months. Females reach reproductive maturity at around 18 months, and males reach maturity a little earlier but will not mate until they can participate in the rut (fight for mates) at age 3 or 4.

Predators: Wolves, coyotes, bears, bobcats, mountain lions, and humans

Tracks: Both front and hind feet have two teardrop- or comma-shaped toes.

Mule deer have large ears and are overall brownish gray with a white patch of fur on their rump and a black-tipped white tail.

Did you know?

The raccoon is great at catching fish and other aquatic animals, such as mussels and crayfish. They are also excellent swimmers, but they apparently avoid swimming because the water makes their fur heavy. Raccoons can turn their feet 180 degrees; this helps them when climbing, especially when going headfirst down trees.

Size Comparison   Most Active   Track Size   Hibernates

Northern Raccoon

Procyon lotor

Size: 24–40 inches long; weighs 15–28 pounds

Habitat: Woody areas, grasslands, suburban and urban areas, wetlands, and marshes

Range: They are found throughout the US; they are also found in Mexico and southern Canada. In Arizona, they are common statewide.

Food: Eggs, insects, garbage, garden plants, berries, nuts, fish, carrion, small mammals, and aquatic invertebrates like crayfish and mussels

Den: Raccoon dens are built in hollow trees, abandoned burrows, caves, and human-made structures.

Young: 2–6 young (kits) are born around March through July. They are born weighing 2 ounces, are around 4 inches long, and are blind with lightly colored fur.

Predators: Coyotes, foxes, bobcats, humans, and even large birds of prey

Tracks: Their front tracks resemble human handprints. The back tracks sort of look like human footprints.

The northern raccoon has dense fur with variations of brown, black, and white streaks. It has black, mask-like markings on its face and a black-and-gray/brownish ringed tail. During the fall, it will grow a thick layer of fat to stay warm in the winter.

Did you know?

The pronghorn is the fastest land animal in North America. It can reach speeds of 60 miles per hour and jump over 20 feet in distance. The pronghorn is only found in North America. Though it looks similar to an antelope, it is not related. They are more closely related to giraffes!

Size Comparison   Most Active   Track Size

2¾"

Pronghorn

Antilocapra americana

Size: 4½ feet long; 3½ feet to shoulder; weighs 90–150 pounds

Habitat: Grasslands, shrublands, mixed-grass prairies, brushlands, and deserts

Range: The pronghorn can be found throughout much of the western United States, down into Mexico, and northward into southern Canada. There are three subspecies in Arizona: The American subspecies is found in the northern half, while the other two species (the Sonoran and desert) are found in the southwestern and southeastern portions.

Food: They are herbivores that eat grasses and sagebrush.

Den: No den; will bed in grass and use tall grass to hide young (fawns)

Young: Usually give birth to 1–2 fawns. They are able to stand within a few hours. The fawns will join the herd when they are about a week old and begin grazing when they are 3 weeks old. Fawns stay with their mother for about a year until they become independent.

Predators: Mountain lions, wolves, coyotes, bears, and eagles

Track: Front tracks are about 3¼ inches long, while the hind tracks are about 2¾ inches long.

Pronghorns are reddish tan to brown in color. They have a white rump, belly, chest, and cheeks. The inside of their legs is also white. Males have a black mask that extends down the face from their eyes to their nose. Males have large horns that curve inward. Females have smaller horns that are usually straight; they do not have black markings on their face.

Did you know?

Ringtails are also called civet cats, ringtail cats, and miner's cats, although they are not related to cats. They are related to raccoons! Their ankles can rotate 180 degrees, which allows them to go headfirst down a cliff or tree.

Size Comparison   Most Active   Track Size

1—1½"

Ringtail

Bassariscus astutus

Size: 24 inches long (half is tail); weighs 1½–2 pounds

Habitat: Canyons, rocky outcrops, deserts, woodlands, montane forests (forests in mountains), and shrublands

Range: They are found in the southwestern US to Texas and in northern Mexico. In Arizona, they can be found in many areas across the state, though they are rarely seen due to their secretive lifestyle.

Food: They are omnivores that eat fruit, insects, birds, flowers, small mammals, carrion (dead animals), seeds, amphibians, grains, bird eggs, reptiles, and nuts.

Den: Dens are usually in hollow trees, rock crevices, or boulder piles. They will also den in human structures. Dens are usually lined with grasses, moss, or leaves.

Young: Young are born blind and naked. Their eyes do not open until around day 30 or so when they start to eat solid food. They are weaned from milk around 2½ months. At around 10 months, they will reach reproductive maturity.

Predators: Bobcats, coyotes, and great horned owls

Tracks: Front feet are 1–1¾ inches long and 1¼–1½ inches wide. Hind feet are 1–1½ inches long and ¾–1¼ inches wide. Tracks have five toes.

Ringtails have a catlike body that is yellowish gray to black on their back and buffy gray on their belly. They have large ears, a pointed muzzle, and long whiskers. Their face has a black-to-brown-patterned mask with white-to-buffy eye rings. They have a long, buffy-colored tail that is separated by seven black rings.

Did you know?

Skunks help farmers! They save farmers money by feeding on rodents and insects that destroy crops. When skunks spray, they can aim really well! When threatened, a skunk will aim its tail towards the threat and spray a stinky musk into the target's face or eyes.

Size Comparison	Most Active	Track Size	Hibernates
		1½"	

Striped Skunk

Mephitis mephitis

Size: 17–30 inches long; weighs 6–13 pounds

Habitat: Woodlands, prairies, and suburban areas

Range: Found throughout Arizona, minus the extreme desert areas; they can be found throughout the US and into Canada and the northern parts of Mexico.

Food: Omnivores (eaters of meat and plants), they eat eggs, fruits, nuts, small mammals, carrion (dead things), insects, amphibians, small reptiles, and even garbage.

Den: Skunks prefer short and shallow natural dens, or dens abandoned by other animals, but will dig dens 3–6 feet long and up to 3 feet deep underground. Dens have multiple hidden entrances, and rooms are usually lined with vegetation.

Young: They have 4–5 young (kits) that are blind at birth; at around 3 weeks they gain vision and the ability to spray.

Predators: Raptors and large carnivores

Tracks: Their front feet have five long, curved claws used for digging; the hind foot also has five toes and is longer and skinnier than the front foot.

The striped skunk is a cat-size, nocturnal (active at night) mammal with black fur and two white stripes that run the entire length of the body. The stripe pattern is usually distinctive to each skunk.

Did you know?

The white-nosed coati is not a raccoon, but it is in the same family. Coatis will sometimes travel over a mile in a day in search of food, often using their tail to aid in balance.

Size Comparison   Most Active   Track Size

2¼–3"

White-nosed Coati
Nasua narica

Size: 25 inches long; weighs 5½–15 pounds

Habitat: Grasslands, open forests, mountainous forests, woody canyons, and tropical woodlands

Range: They can be found from South America northward through Mexico into Texas, New Mexico, and Arizona. In Arizona, they are found from the southern portion to the central area of the state.

Food: Insects, frogs, small mammals, lizards, and fruit

Den: They sleep in the tops of trees; females will build a much more robust nest in a treetop to have kits.

Young: Usually 2–7 kits are born with their eyes closed after a 2½-month pregnancy. Young open eyes at around day 11 and are weaned at around 4 months. They reach reproductive maturity at around 2 years for females and 3 years for males.

Predators: Large cats, birds of prey, humans, foxes, and snakes

Tracks: Front tracks are 2¼–3¼ inches long and 1¼–2 inches wide. Rear feet are 2¼–3 inches long and 1⅜–2 inches wide.

Coatis have small heads with a long, pointed snout or nose. They have small ears and a long tail. They have sharp claws and sport a black- or brownish-and-white mask around their eyes and nose. They have brown-to-burnt-red fur with a mixture of white and yellow on their back. Their underside is lighter brown to tannish in color. Males are larger than females.

Did you know?

The American kestrel is the smallest species of falcon not only in the US but in all of North America! It's also the most common falcon of North America.

Nest Type   Most Active

58

American Kestrel

Falco sparverius

Size: 8½–12¼ inches long; wingspan of 20 inches; weight: 2¾–6 ounces

Habitat: Cities, suburbs, forests, and open areas such as meadows, grasslands, deserts, parks, and farm fields

Range: They can be found throughout most of North America, except the extreme north of Canada and Alaska. In Arizona, they are common statewide as year-round residents.

Food: Grasshoppers, dragonflies, small birds, lizards, and mice; sometimes snakes, bats, and squirrels

Nesting: Nest in cavities that are made by other birds like woodpeckers, in human-made and natural crevices like tree hollows, and in crevices of rock formations

Nest: They do not use nesting materials but will make a small depression if material is already present.

Eggs: 4–5 yellowish-to-white or burnt-red-brown eggs, 1–1½ inches long and 1 inch wide

Young: Chicks hatch 25–33 days after laying and will leave the nest around 30 days later. Chicks hatch with pink skin and little down feathers.

Predators: Snakes; large birds of prey, like hawks, owls, and crows; bobcats, skunks, and other mammals

Migration: Not a migrant in Arizona

Kestrels sport a rusty-brown, spotted back. Their tail has a black band that stretches across it. Females have brown-to-reddish wings, and the males have grayish-blue wings. Both males and females have black lines under their eyes that resemble mascara or makeup running down their face.

Did you know?

The bald eagle is an endangered species success story! The bald eagle was once endangered due to a pesticide called DDT that weakened eggshells and caused them to crack early. Through the banning of DDT and other conservation efforts, the bald eagle population recovered, and it was removed from the Endangered Species List in July of 2007.

Nest Type

Most Active

Migrates

Bald Eagle

Haliaeetus leucocephalus

Size: 3½ feet long; wingspan of 6½–8 feet; weighs 8–14 pounds

Habitat: Forests and tree stands (small forests) near river edges, lakes, seashores, and wetlands

Range: They are nonbreeding residents throughout much of Arizona and year-round residents in a few areas of the central part of the state; they are found throughout much of the US.

Food: Fish, waterfowl (ducks), rabbits, squirrels, muskrats, and deer carcasses; will steal food from other eagles or osprey

Nesting: Eagles have lifelong partners that begin nesting in fall, laying eggs between November–February.

Nest: They build a large nest out of sticks, high up in trees; the nest can be over 5 feet wide and over 6 feet tall, often shaped like an upside-down cone.

Eggs: 1–3 white eggs

Young: Young (chicks) will hatch at around 35 days; young will leave the nest at around 12 weeks. It takes up to 5 years for eagles to get that iconic look!

Predators: Few; collisions with cars sometimes occur.

Migration: Many migrate to Arizona during the nonbreeding season of winter and will travel north during the spring.

Adult bald eagles have a dark-brown body, a white head and tail, and a golden-yellow beak. Juvenile eagles are mostly brown at first, but their color pattern changes over their first few years. A bald eagle can use its wings as oars to propel itself across bodies of water.

Did you know?

Burrowing owls are fossorial, meaning that they live and/or spend most of their day underground. They will sometimes mimic rattlesnakes when threatened, by hiding in a burrow and making rattling and hissing sounds. They like to decorate their mounds with scat, or poop, from mammals. It is believed that the scat helps to attract insects to eat and to hide the scent of the owl's young.

Nest Type	Most Active	Migrates

Burrowing Owl

Athene cunicularia

Size: 7½–11 inches long; wingspan of 20–22 inches; weighs 5–6 ounces

Habitat: Savanna forest, urban and suburban areas, farmlands, shrublands, prairies, deserts, and mountains

Range: They can be found from southern Canada down into Mexico and as far east as Minnesota and Texas. In Arizona, they are breeding residents in the northern portion of the state and year-round residents in the southern half.

Food: Carnivores; mostly insects and rodents, but also amphibians, reptiles, birds, and rarely seeds and fruit

Nesting: March to April

Nest: Nests in burrows usually made by other animals. The male will line the nesting burrow with plants, feathers, scat, and sometimes trash.

Eggs: 4–12 white eggs often tinted the color of the dirt

Young: Owlets hatch 3–4 weeks after laying. Within 4 weeks, they are able to fly short distances and explore areas outside of the burrow. They will receive care for another 1–3 months until they can hunt.

Predators: Snakes, pet cats and dogs, foxes, skunks, hawks, falcons, weasels, and other owl species; humans play a heavy role in displacement and loss of habitat.

Migration: Northern populations will migrate, while populations in the southern part do not.

Burrowing owls are small, brown owls adorned by white spots of various sizes on their back. They have a white or creamy belly with brown bars. They have large yellow eyes with thick white eyebrows and throat.

63

Did you know?
The cactus wren is the largest wren in the United States! They get their name from living on cacti.

Nest Type

Most Active

Cactus Wren

Campylorhynchus brunneicapillus

Size: 7–8¾ inches long; wingspan of 11 inches; weighs 1–1¾ ounces

Habitat: Deserts, arid foothills, coastal sage scrublands, and urban (city) areas

Range: They can be found in the western part of North America, from California to Texas and down into Mexico. They can be found as year-round residents from the western portion of Arizona through the central part of the state and southward.

Food: They are omnivores that mostly eat insects and spiders, as well as small reptiles, fruits, and berries.

Nesting: February–March

Nest: The football-shaped nest is built on a cactus. They will use the nest during breeding and nonbreeding seasons.

Eggs: 2–7 pinkish-to-buff-colored eggs with reddish or brown spots on them

Young: 16–17 days after laying, the chicks will hatch with eyes closed and almost naked, except for patches of fluffy white feathers. They will fledge after 17–23 days.

Predators: Snakes, coyotes, bobcats, pet cats, hawks, and foxes

Migration: Does not migrate

Adult cactus wrens are large and have a long bill and tail. They have a cream-colored breast with brown-and-black spotting. Their short wings have bar patterns that include brown, black, and white. They have a white stripe behind each eye. Juveniles are lighter in color and have brown-gray eyes.

Did you know?

The elf owl is the world's smallest raptor and owl! They are about the size of a juice box or a sparrow. When caught by predators, they will play dead until the coast is clear.

Nest Type   Most Active   Migrates

Elf Owl

Micrathene whitneyi

Size: 4¾–5½ inches long; wingspan of 13 inches; weighs 1¼–2 ounces

Habitat: Forests, deserts, shrublands, woodlands, canyons, and savannas

Range: Breeding residents, they can be found in the southern half of Arizona, as well as the southwestern portion of North America, including New Mexico, Texas, and Mexico.

Food: Carnivores, they eat mostly insects, small mammals, and reptiles.

Nesting: Spring, mid-March–early May

Nest: They nest in old woodpecker holes, in cacti, or on telephone poles.

Eggs: 1–5 (usually 3) white eggs are laid per clutch.

Young: 24 days after laying, hatchlings will hatch covered with thick white down. Young will leave the nest at around a month and will reach reproductive maturity within a year.

Predators: Other owls, coyotes, snakes, ringtails, and bobcats

Migration: In Arizona, they are breeding residents that migrate to Mexico in the fall.

Elf owls are small birds with short tails; large, round ear tufts; rounded wings; and small feet. They are brown and black with areas of white throughout their bodies and thin black framing around their faces. They have yellow eyes with thin white streaks above them that resemble eyebrows. They have a gray bill and a small head compared to their body size.

The Gila woodpecker (pronounced he-la) is named after the Gila River, which flows through Arizona. Their abandoned nesting cavities are used by other birds. The cavities that they dig in Saguaro cacti are called boots.

Nest Type Most Active

Gila Woodpecker

Melanerpes uropygialis

Size: 9¼ inches long; wingspan of 16 inches; weighs 2¼ ounces

Habitat: Forests, urban areas, shrublands, deserts, and other arid areas

Range: They are found in southwestern North America in Arizona, California, Nevada, New Mexico, and Mexico. In Arizona, they are found in the southwestern and southern areas of the state as year-round residents.

Food: Omnivores, they feed on insects, fruits, seeds, small lizards, birds, and even eggs.

Mating: April–May

Nest: Cavity in a cactus or tree

Eggs: 3–4 white eggs per brood, with the possibility to have 2–3 broods per season. Eggs are incubated by both parents.

Young: Young hatch 13–14 days after laying, naked and dependent on parents. Young fledge at around 4 weeks after hatching.

Predators: Snakes, foxes, bobcats, coyotes, hawks, and pet cats

Migration: Does not migrate

Gila woodpeckers are medium-size birds. Their wings and back have black-and-white patterns of spotting and bars similar to the red-bellied woodpeckers. The breast, neck, belly, and head are a gray-tan color. The males' heads are red on top, and females' and juveniles' heads are brown. Females and juveniles look similar. All Gila woodpeckers have white wing patches that are visible while in flight.

Did you know?

Golden eagles are the largest bird of prey that actively hunts in North America! They are North America's second-largest bird of prey after the California condor, which is a scavenger. Golden eagles also have the widest range of all eagles. They can be found across North America, Africa, Europe, and Asia. Several countries have named the golden eagle as their national bird, including Mexico, Albania, Kazakhstan, and Austria.

Nest Type   Most Active

Golden Eagle

Aquila chrysaetos

Size: 26–33 inches long; wingspan of 6–8 feet; weighs 7½–9 pounds

Habitat: Shrublands, forests, mountains, cliffs, canyons, grasslands, rocky areas, and woodlands

Range: Widespread across North America throughout various seasons. In Arizona, they are year-round residents.

Food: Birds, goats, sheep, coyotes, pronghorns, badgers, reptiles, deer, fish, bobcats, and small mammals

Nesting: January–May

Nest: Nests on cliffs, trees, and buildings. Nests are made of sticks and other plant materials; they will sometimes include animal bones and human objects.

Eggs: 2–3 cream-to-light-pink eggs are laid.

Young: Eaglets hatch about 40–45 days after eggs are laid. They learn to fly at around 10 weeks. They will reproduce at around 4–7 years.

Predators: Humans are often the cause of death due to habitat loss and hunting practices.

Migration: Year-round residents in Arizona

Golden eagles are covered in dark-brown feathers. They have a golden neck and sides of their face, which is where they get their name. They have broad wings that stretch over 7 feet across. The tail is faded brown to dark brown. They have deep-brown eyes, a black-tipped bill, and black claws. Their feet are yellow, and their legs are covered with feathers. Immature eagles have patches of white-to-buffy-colored feathers.

Did you know?

The great blue heron is the largest and most common heron species. A heron's eye color changes as it ages. The eyes start out gray but transition to yellow over time. Great blue herons swallow their prey whole.

Nest Type   Most Active   Migrates

Great Blue Heron

Ardea herodias

Size: 3–4½ feet long; wingspan of 6–7 feet; weighs 5–7 pounds

Habitat: Lakes, ponds, rivers, marshes, lagoons, wetlands

Range: They can be found throughout the United States and down into Mexico. In Arizona, they are year-round residents in most of the state, with a migrating population in the western corner that borders Nevada and California.

Food: Fish, rats, crabs, shrimp, grasshoppers, crayfish, other birds, small mammals, snakes, and lizards

Nesting: May–August

Nest: 2–3 feet across and saucer shaped; often grouped in large rookeries (colonies) in tall trees along the water's edge. Nests are built out of sticks and are often located in dead trees more than 100 feet above the ground; nests are used year after year.

Eggs: 3–7 pale bluish eggs

Young: Chicks will hatch after 28 days of incubation; young will stay in the nest for around 10 weeks. They reach reproductive maturity at just under 2 years.

Predators: Eagles, crows, gulls, raccoons, bears, and hawks

Migration: Populations in the western part of the state migrate, while the rest are year-round residents.

The great blue heron is a large wading bird with blue and gray upper body feathers; the belly area is white. They have long yellow legs that they use to stalk prey in the water. Great blue herons are famous for stalking prey at the water's edge; their specially adapted feet keep them from sinking into the mud!

Did you know?

A great horned owl can exert a crushing force of over 300 pounds with its talons. Despite its name, the great horned owl doesn't have horns at all. Instead, the obvious tufts on its head are made of feathers. Scientists aren't sure exactly how the tufts function, but they may help them stay hidden.

Nest Type   Most Active

Great Horned Owl

Bubo virginianus

Size: Up to 23 inches long; wingspan of 45 inches; weighs 3 pounds

Habitat: Woods; swamps; desert edges; as well as heavily populated areas such as cities, suburbs, and parks

Range: They are found throughout the continent of North America. They are year-round residents in Arizona.

Food: They eat a variety of foods, but mostly mammals. Sometimes they eat other birds as well.

Nesting: They have lifelong partnerships, with nesting season starting in early winter; egg-laying starts in mid-January to February.

Nest: Nests are found 20–50 feet off the ground. They tend to reuse nests from other raptors or hollowed-out trees.

Eggs: The female lays 2–4 whitish eggs. Eggs are incubated for around 30 days.

Young: Young can fly at around 9 weeks old. The parents care for and feed young for several months.

Predators: Young owls are preyed upon by foxes, coyotes, bears, and opossums. As adults, they are rarely attacked by other birds of prey, such as golden eagles and goshawks.

Migration: Great horned owls are not regular migrators, but some individuals will travel south during the winter.

They are bulky birds with large ear tufts, a rusty brown-to-grayish face with a black border, and large bright eyes. The body color tends to be brown; the wing pattern is checkered with an intermingled dark brown. The chest and belly areas are light brown and have white bars.

Did you know?

Great-tailed grackles are smart birds; they can use their problem-solving skills to solve puzzles! They can flock in numbers that exceed 2,000 birds. In many places, they are just called blackbirds and will often mix in with other birds, including true blackbirds. Great-tailed grackles will defend their nests by diving, chasing, and mobbing would-be predators—and even humans who wander too close.

Nest Type   Most Active

Great-tailed Grackle

Quiscalus mexicanus

Size: 15–18 inches long; wingspan of 19–22¾ inches; weighs 4–9¼ ounces

Habitat: Wetlands, coastal areas, suburban areas, fields, forests, and grasslands

Range: They are found from South America northward into Mexico and the southern and midwestern states west of the Mississippi. They are year-round residents found throughout Arizona.

Food: They are omnivores that feed on lizards, eggs, birds, insects, berries, fish, worms, and other invertebrates.

Nesting: April

Nest: They make a cup nest with grass, twigs, and man-made materials.

Eggs: 4–7 eggs

Young: Chicks hatch 14 days or so after laying, naked and with their eyes closed. They fledge from the nest at around 15 days and receive food from the parents for several more weeks. They reach reproductive maturity at around 1–2 years.

Predators: Hawks, owls, pet cats, raccoons, snakes, and squirrels

Migration: Does not migrate

Male great-tailed grackles are iridescent shades of black with bluish-green-and-purple feathers on their upper body and head. Females are brown and duller with darker wings and tails. Adults have bright-yellow eyes, while juveniles have brown eyes.

Did you know?

The greater roadrunner can run over 15 miles per hour! It is so quick that it can grab dragonflies and hummingbirds from mid-air! Its quick speed also allows it to hunt and eat rattlesnakes.

Nest Type   Most Active

Greater Roadrunner

Geococcyx californianus

Size: 20½–21¼ inches; wingspan of 19¼ inches; weighs 17¾–19 ounces

Habitat: Scrubby habitats, deserts, brushlands, grasslands, and forest edges

Range: They're found across the western United States from Missouri to California. In Arizona, they are in the majority of the state, except for the eastern corner.

Food: Snakes, rodents, insects, scorpions, lizards, small birds, and sometimes fruits and seeds

Nesting: March to late-October

Nest: They build their nests in dense brush, cacti, or trees. Nests are platforms made of sticks and lined with grass, feathers, and leaves.

Eggs: 3–5 white-to-light-yellow eggs that sometimes have brown or gray stains, usually 1–2 clutches per year

Young: 19–20 days after laying, the chicks hatch with eyes closed and with white down and black skin. They will fledge from the nest at around 20 days. They reach reproductive maturity at around 2–3 years old.

Predators: Coyotes, hawks, raccoons, and pet cats

Migration: They do not migrate.

Roadrunners are medium-size, slender birds with a tan-and-brown body. Their chest and underside are streaked with black and brown. Their crown or top of the head is black with small spots of white and paler browns. They have dark wings that are highlighted by white. They have a long tail and legs.

Did you know?

Downy woodpeckers are the smallest woodpecker species in North America. Hairy woodpeckers can hear insects traveling under the tree bark. Downy woodpeckers have a built-in mask, or special feathers, near their nostrils that helps them to avoid breathing in wood chips while pecking.

Nest Type   Most Active

Hairy/Downy Woodpecker

Leuconotopicus villosus/Dryobates pubescens

Size: Hairy: 7–10 inches long; wingspan of 13–16 inches; weighs 3 ounces. Downy: 5½–7 inches long; wingspan of 10–12 inches; weighs less than an ounce

Habitat: Forested areas, parks, woodlands, and orchards

Range: Hairy: in much of the US, and can be found in ¾ of the state in northwestern and eastern Arizona. Downy: found in the eastern quarter of the state.

Food: Hairy: beetles, ants, caterpillars, fruits, and seeds. Downy: beetles, ants, galls, wasps, seeds, and berries

Nesting: Hairy: March to June. Downy: January to March

Nest: In both woodpecker species, pairs will work together to create a cavity. Both parents also help to incubate eggs.

Eggs: Hairy: 3–7 white eggs. Downy: 3–8 white eggs

Young: Hairy woodpeckers' eggs will hatch 2 weeks after being laid and then fledge (develop enough feathers to fly) after another month. Downy woodpeckers' eggs will hatch after about 12 days and fledge 18–21 days after hatching. Both species hatch blind and featherless.

Predators: American kestrels, snakes, sharp-shinned hawks, pet cats, rats, squirrels, and Cooper's hawks

Migration: Woodpeckers are mostly year-round residents.

Hairy woodpeckers and downy woodpeckers look strikingly similar with their color pattern. One way to distinguish them is to look at the size of the body and bill. The downy woodpecker is smaller than the hairy woodpecker and has a shorter bill. If you look at the tail feathers of the two species, you will also see that the hairy woodpecker does not have black spots, while the downy's tail does.

Did you know?

Harris's hawks are the only birds of prey that hunt in groups! Cooperative hunting groups allow them to be more successful than when hunting alone. These social birds also use a behavior called stacking that allows them to see predators or prey better.

Nest Type   Most Active

Harris's Hawk

Parabuteo unicinctus

Size: 18–23¼ inches long; wingspan of 40½–47 inches; weighs 18¼–31 ounces

Habitat: Deserts, wetlands, woodlands, forests, urban and suburban areas, and savannas

Range: They can be found in the southwestern corner of North America in Arizona, New Mexico, Texas, and Mexico. They are found along the western and eastern portions of the state, from central Arizona southward.

Food: Rodents, birds, rabbits and hares, and reptiles

Nesting: March–June

Nest: They make platform nests out of sticks, weeds, and twigs. The nests are often lined with moss, grass, and roots. They are made in trees, cacti, on cliffs, and even on human-made objects.

Eggs: 2–4 faded-bluish-to-white eggs are laid at a time, with up to 3 clutches possible per year.

Young: A month after laying, chicks will hatch helpless and covered in down feathers. Chicks fledge the nest around 40–48 days after hatching and will stay around the nest for 2–3 months.

Predators: Owls, ravens, and coyotes

Migration: Does not migrate

Harris's hawks are large with long wings and tails. Adults are a dark brown overall with reddish shoulders, underwings, and legs. Their tail is dark on top with white banding underneath. Juveniles look similar to adults but have a white belly with brown streaking, and their colors are not as distinct on the back. They also have barring on the back side of their tails.

Cardinals are very territorial. A cardinal will sometimes attack its own reflection, thinking that another cardinal has entered its territory. The early bird gets the worm, and cardinals are some of the first birds active in the morning.

Nest Type   Most Active

Northern Cardinal

Cardinalis cardinalis

Size: 8–9 inches long; wingspan of 12 inches

Habitat: Hardwood forests, urban areas, orchards, backyards, and fields

Range: They are found throughout the eastern and midwestern parts of the United States. Arizona is the most western state where you can find them. They are year-round residents in the central and southeastern parts of the state.

Food: Seeds, fruits, insects, spiders, and centipedes

Nesting: March to August

Nest: The cup-shaped nest is built by females in thick foliage, usually at least 1 foot off the ground. It can be 3 inches tall and 4 inches wide.

Eggs: The female lays 2–5 off-white eggs with a variety of colored speckles.

Young: About 2 weeks after eggs are laid, chicks hatch with their eyes closed and mostly naked, aside from sparsely placed down feathers.

Predators: Hawks, owls, and squirrels

Migration: Cardinals do not migrate.

Northern cardinal males are bright-red birds with a black face. Females are a washed-out red or brown. Both males and females have a crest (tuft of feathers on the head), an orange beak, and grayish legs. Cardinals can be identified by their laser-gun-like call.

Did you know?

The osprey is nicknamed the "fish hawk" because it is the only hawk in North America that mainly eats live fish. An osprey will rotate its catch to put it in line with its body, pointing headfirst, which allows for less resistance in flight as the air travels over the fish.

Nest Type   Most Active   Migrates

Osprey

Pandion haliaetus

Size: 21–23 inches long; wingspan of 59–71 inches; weighs 3–4½ pounds

Habitat: Near lakes, ponds, rivers, swamps, and reservoirs

Range: They are found throughout the US. In Arizona, they are found statewide during migration, with some breeding residents in the central portion of the state and winter residents in the southwestern corner.

Food: Feeds mostly on fish; they sometimes eat mammals, birds, and reptiles if there are few fish.

Nesting: For ospreys that migrate, egg-laying happens in April and May. The female will take on most of the incubation of the eggs, as well as the jobs of keeping the offspring warm and providing protection.

Nest: Platform nests are made out of twigs and sticks on trees, snags, or human-made objects.

Eggs: The mother lays 1–3 cream-colored eggs with splotches of browns and pinkish reds.

Young: Chicks hatch after around 36 days and have brown-and-white down feathers. Ospreys fledge around 50–55 days after hatching and will receive care from parents for another 2 months or so.

Predators: Owls, eagles, foxes, skunks, raccoons, and snakes

Migration: Ospreys migrate south to wintering areas in the fall.

Ospreys are raptors, and they have a brown upper body and white lower body. The wings are brown on the outside and white on the underside, with brown spotting and streaks toward the edge. The head is white with a brown band that goes through the eye area, highlighting the yellow eyes.

Did you know?
The peregrine falcon is the fastest diving bird in the world. A peregrine falcon can reach speeds over 200 miles per hour (mph) when diving. To aid in diving and maneuvering in the air, like most other birds, peregrine falcons have a third eyelid called a nictitating membrane that helps to keep out debris and wind.

Nest Type Most Active Migrates

Peregrine Falcon

Falco peregrinus

Size: 14–19½ inches long; wingspan of 39–43 inches; weighs 1–3½ pounds

Habitat: Hardwood forests, coastal areas and marshes, urban areas, orchards, backyards, and fields

Range: In Arizona, a majority are year-round residents, with migrating visitors in the eastern side of the state. They are found throughout North America.

Food: Carnivores, they feed on pigeons, songbirds, aquatic birds, rodents, and sometimes bats.

Nesting: February to March. Pairs mate for life and reuse nests. The female chooses a nest site usually on a cliff edge or tall building. Sometimes they even use abandoned nests of other large birds.

Nest: Shallow ground scrapes about 8–9 inches wide and 2 inches deep with no extra nesting materials added

Eggs: 3–5 off-white-to-brown eggs speckled brown or purple

Young: 30 days after eggs are laid, chicks (or eyas) will hatch with eyes closed and covered in off-white down.

Predators: Great horned owls, golden eagles, and humans

Migration: Falcons in a small area of eastern Arizona migrate for breeding, while falcons in the rest of the state are year-round residents.

The female is slightly larger than the male. Peregrine falcons have gray wings with black-to-gray, bar-like marks and deep-black wing tips. The breast and belly areas are covered with black-to-brown horizontal streaks or bars. They have a black head and black marks below the eyes. The neck is white. The beak, legs, eye rings, and feet are yellow.

Did you know?

The name "phainopepla" has a Greek origin that means "shining robe." Phainopeplas have a built-in mechanism that aids in better digestion, allowing them to eat mistletoe and other berries. In their gizzard, a process occurs that separates the skin from the fruit of the berry. They are the only birds known to be able to do this, which is important because they can eat more than 1,000 berries in a day.

Nest Type	Most Active	Migrates

Phainopepla

Phainopepla nitens

Size: 7–8¼ inches long; wingspan of 10½–11½ inches; weighs ½–1 ounce

Habitat: Forests, shrublands, deserts, canyon bottoms, woodlands, and orchards

Range: They are found in the southwestern portion of North America (from California to western Texas down into Mexico) as breeding residents. In Arizona, they can be found from the center of the state southward; they are breeding residents in the northern part and year-round residents in the southern part of the range.

Food: Omnivores, they eat fruits, berries, insects, and lizards.

Nesting: Spring; the males select the nest site.

Nest: Nests are cup shaped, about 4 inches across and 2 inches high, with the inside cup being 2½ inches wide and 1¼ inches deep.

Eggs: 2–4 round, grayish eggs with dark speckles are laid in a brood.

Young: Young hatch helpless with a small amount of white down on top of grayish-black skin. The nesting period is only about 14–20 days.

Predators: Snakes, birds of prey, bobcats, foxes, coyotes, and pet cats

Migration: Migrates from Mexico to Arizona to breed

Male phainopeplas are adorned in a silky black plumage. They have a head crest, red eyes, and white wing patches that are visible in flight. Females and juveniles are duller in color; adult females have red eyes, while juveniles have brownish eyes. Phainopeplas are overall slender birds with long tails and short bills.

The red-tailed hawk is the most abundant hawk in North America. The red-tailed hawk's scream is the sound effect that you hear when soaring eagles are shown in movies. Eagles do not screech like hawks, so filmmakers use hawk calls instead! Red-tailed hawks can't move their eyes, so they have to move their entire head in order to get a better view around them.

Nest Type   Most Active

Red-tailed Hawk

Buteo jamaicensis

Size: 19–25 inches long; wingspan of 47–57 inches; weighs 2½–4 pounds

Habitat: Deserts, woodlands, grasslands, and farm fields

Range: Throughout North America; in Arizona, they are year-round residents throughout the state.

Food: Rodents, birds, reptiles, amphibians, bats, and insects

Nesting: Hawks mate for life; nesting starts in March.

Nest: Both the male and female help build a large cup-shaped nest, which can be over 6 feet high and 3 feet across; the nest is made of sticks and branches; nests are built at forest edges mostly in the crowns of trees, but hawks will also nest on windowsills and other human-made structures.

Eggs: 1–5 eggs; the insides of eggs are a greenish color.

Young: They start to fly after 5–6 weeks, and it takes around 10 weeks for the hatchlings to leave the nest.

Predators: Great-horned owls and crows

Migration: Does not migrate

Red-tailed hawks are named for their rusty-red tails! They have brown heads and a chest that's cream to light brown with brown streaking in the form of a band. Red-tailed hawks are highly territorial, and throughout the day they will take to the air to look for invaders.

Did you know?

Red-winged blackbirds are one of the most abundant songbirds in the United States. Sometimes their winter roost (colony) can have several thousand to up to a million birds. In many areas, red-winged blackbirds are considered a pest because of their love of grain and seeds from farm fields. In others, they are welcomed because they eat insects that are considered pests to farmers.

Nest Type   Most Active

Red-winged Blackbird

Agelaius phoeniceus

Size: 7–9½ inches long; wingspan of 13 inches; weighs 2 ounces

Habitat: Marshes, lakeshores, meadows, parks, and open fields

Range: Throughout Arizona as year-round residents; ranges from central Canada through the US and into Mexico

Food: Dragonflies, spiders, beetles, snails, seeds, and fruits

Nesting: February to August

Nest: Female builds a cup from plant material.

Eggs: 3–4 eggs that come in a variety of colors, from pale blue to gray with black-and-brown spots or streaks

Young: Chicks hatch blind and naked after around 12 days of incubation. Hatchlings will leave the nest after 12 days but will continue to receive care for another 5 weeks.

Predators: Raccoons, mink, marsh wrens, and raptors

Migration: Arizona populations do not migrate.

Red-winged blackbird males are a sleek black with an orangish-red spot that overlays a dandelion-yellow spot on the wings. Females have a combination of dark-brown and light-brown streaks throughout the body. Male red-winged blackbirds spend much of breeding season defending their territory from other males and attacking predators or anything else that gets too close to the nest.

Did you know?

The Say's phoebe has an expansive breeding range, from the Arctic tundra of Alaska south to central Mexico. Say's phoebes will nest in many human-made places like mailboxes and mines. They often reuse their nests multiple years in a row.

Nest Type   Most Active   Migrates

Say's Phoebe

Sayornis saya

Size: 6¾ inches long; wingspan of 13 inches; weighs ¾ ounce

Habitat: Open country, grasslands, sagebrush, shrublands, foothills, canyons, and borders of deserts

Range: They are found throughout western North America from Alaska down through Canada and into Washington and eastward as far as Texas. In Arizona, they are breeding residents in the central-to-eastern parts of the state and year-round residents throughout the rest of the state.

Food: Carnivores, they eat insects, spiders, some fruits, and berries.

Nesting: April–August

Nest: Females build a cup-shaped nest out of plant stems, sage, wood, grasses, and spiderwebs. Rocks are sometimes used in the formation of the nest. Nests are lined with wool, paper, feathers, and hair.

Eggs: 3–6 white eggs are laid per brood.

Young: Chicks hatch about 12–18 days after laying and will fledge within 12–21 days after hatching.

Predators: Owls, hawks, bobcats, coyotes, other birds, pet cats, and snakes

Migration: Birds in the northeastern corner of the state migrate south in the fall and north in the spring for breeding.

Adult Say's phoebes are small with a brown-gray back and cinnamon-buffy-colored underside that turns orange to reddish towards the base of the tail. They have a black tail and long wings. The juvenile has light-orange-buff-to-white armbars that distinguish it from the adults.

97

Did you know?

Turkeys sometimes fly at night, unlike most birds, and land in trees to roost. Turkeys have some interesting facial features; the red skin growth on a turkey's face above the beak is called a snood, while the growth under the beak is called a wattle. Wild turkeys can have more than 5,000 feathers.

Nest Type

Most Active

Wild Turkey

Meleagris gallopavo

Size: 3–4 feet long; wingspan of 5 feet; males weigh 16–25 pounds; females weigh 9–11 pounds

Habitat: Woodlands and grasslands

Range: They can be found in the eastern US and have been introduced in many western areas of the country. They are year-round residents throughout much of the state of Arizona.

Food: Grain, snakes, frogs, insects, acorns, berries, and ferns

Nesting: April to September

Nest: The nest is built on the ground using leaves as bedding, in brush or near the base of trees or fallen logs.

Eggs: 10–12 tan eggs with very small reddish-brown spots

Young: Poults (young) hatch about a month after eggs are laid; they will flock with the mother for a year. When young are still unable to fly, the mom will stay on the ground with her poults to provide protection and warmth. When poults grow up, they are known as a hen if they are female, or a gobbler or tom if they are male.

Predators: Humans, foxes, raccoons, owls, eagles, and skunks

Migration: Turkeys do not migrate.

A wild turkey is a large bird that is dark brown and black with some iridescent feathers. Males will fan out their tail to attract a mate. When threatened, they will also fan out their tail and rush the predator, sometimes kicking and puncturing prey with the spurs on their feet.

Did you know?

Wood ducks will "mimic" a soccer player when a predator is near their young: they flop! Female wood ducks will fake a broken wing to lure predators away from their young. Wood duck hatchlings must jump from the nest after hatching to reach the water. They can jump 50 feet or more without hurting themselves.

Nest Type   Most Active   Migrates

Wood Duck

Aix sponsa

Size: 15–20 inches long; wingspan of 30 inches; weighs about 1 pound

Habitat: Swamps, woody ponds, and marshes

Range: They are nonbreeding residents in central Arizona and eastward; they are also in the eastern US, southern Mexico, the Pacific Northwest, and on the West Coast.

Food: Fruits, nuts, and aquatic vegetation, especially duckweed, sedges, and grasses

Nesting: March to August

Nest: Wood ducks use hollow trees, abandoned woodpecker cavities, and human-made nesting boxes.

Eggs: 8–15 off-white eggs are laid once a year. Sometimes females will lay eggs in another female's nest; this process is called egg dumping.

Young: Eggs hatch about a month after being laid. Chicks will leave the nest after a day and fly within 8 weeks.

Predators: Raccoons, mink, fish, hawks, snapping turtles, owls, humans, and muskrats

Migration: They are nonbreeding residents in Arizona and migrate to breeding areas during the spring.

Wood duck males have a brightly colored crest (tuft of feathers) of iridescent (shimmering) green, red, and purple, with a mahogany (brown) upper breast area and tan bottom. Males also have red eyes. Females are brown to gray. Wood ducks have strong claws that enable them to climb up trees into cavities.

Did you know?
The Arizona tree frog is the state amphibian of Arizona! They are really good climbers and have been found in trees over 70 feet high. Males can be heard calling from the treetops during the breeding season.

Most Active   Hibernates

Arizona Tree Frog

Dryophytes wrightorum

Size: ¾–2 inches long; weighs about as much as a quarter

Habitat: Meadows, forests, mountain streams, ponds, and livestock yards

Range: They are found in western New Mexico and central Arizona, with an isolated population in the southern part of the state.

Food: Carnivores, they eat insects, earthworms, and spiders.

Mating: Summer, during monsoon season

Nest: Does not have a true nest

Eggs: Females lay loose clusters of egg masses attached to vegetation in shallow pools, ponds, and slower-moving streams.

Young: Tadpoles go through metamorphosis (turn into frogs) about 6–11 weeks after hatching.

Predators: Tiger salamander larva, other frogs, and large fish

The Arizona tree frog is a small green frog with dark eye stripes that extend from the snout through the eyes and down the side of the body. The male has a tan or faded-green throat and is smaller than the female. Both sexes are overall green in color on their back with a paler white-to-light-brown tint.

Did you know?
While it resembles a rattlesnake, the Chihuahuan nightsnake is not one and is only mildly venomous. When threatened, it will coil itself and vibrate its tail. Its fangs are in the back of its mouth.

Most Active   Hibernates

Chihuahuan Nightsnake

Hypsiglena jani

Size: 12–16 inches long; weighs 1–3 pounds

Habitat: Grasslands, savannas, shrublands, woodlands, deserts, mountains, and meadows

Range: They are found from Mexico north into the southwestern United States in California, Colorado, Utah, Nevada, Texas, and Arizona, as well as a few midwestern states. This snake can be found across eastern Arizona.

Food: They are carnivores that eat eggs, insects, amphibians, reptiles, and carrion.

Mating: Spring

Nest: Eggs are laid under a rocky crevice or dug-out burrow.

Eggs: 2–6 eggs are laid per clutch.

Young: Young hatch fully independent 50–60 days after laying and are about 6 inches long.

Predators: Hawks, owls, and raccoons

The Chihuahuan nightsnake is a small tan-orangish or gray snake. They have a row of dark-brown blotches that run down their back and three large, dark-colored blotches at the base of their head, making a collar. Each eye has a dark streak that extends to the collar. Their belly is pale gray. They have vertical or elliptical pupils. They hibernate during the winter and fall.

Did you know?

The desert iguana is in the same family as the green iguanas that are found in tropical places like Mexico and South America. They have a high heat tolerance and oftentimes will be the only lizard out during the hotter parts of the day, even in temperatures that are above 110 degrees.

Most Active   Hibernates

Desert Iguana

Dipsosaurus dorsalis

Size: 24 inches long; weighs 2–3 ounces

Habitat: Forests, grasslands, and shrublands

Range: They are found in the southwestern corner of North America in California, Arizona, and Mexico. In Arizona, they are found in the southwestern and northwestern corners and the central portion of the state.

Food: They are herbivores that mainly eat fruits, leaves, insects, and sometimes carrion (dead animals).

Mating: Spring and early summer

Nest: Burrow dug in the ground

Eggs: A clutch of 3–8 eggs is laid per year.

Young: Young hatch around September and are independent at hatching. They will reach maturity at 3 years old.

Predators: Birds of prey, snakes, foxes, and coyotes

The desert iguana is a large gray-cream or tan lizard. They have a brown, reticulated (interlaced or mesh-looking) pattern down their back. Their tail has brown stipes along it, and their belly is pale. Both sexes' sides turn pink during the breeding season. They have a thick head, long tail, and short limbs.

Did you know?
The desert rosy boa is a member of the *Boidae* family, the same family that includes large boas and giant anacondas. The rosy boa is one of the smallest snakes in the boa family and is one of four species that are native to the US.

Most Active   Hibernates

Desert Rosy Boa

Lichanura trivirgata

Size: 16¾–44 inches long; weighs 1 pound

Habitat: Caves, mountains, rocky areas, shrublands, forests, and wetlands

Range: They are found in the southwestern United States in California and Arizona, as well as in northwestern Mexico. In Arizona, they are found in the western portion of the state that borders California.

Food: Small mammals and birds

Mating: Spring

Nest: Gives birth in a burrow or under rocks

Eggs: No eggs; gives live birth

Young: Females give birth to about 6 snakelets in a brood; they are 12 inches long and are independent at birth. Young usually reach reproductive maturity at 2–3 years of age.

Predators: Snakes, birds of prey, raccoons, ringtails, skunks, and coyotes

Desert rosy boas are small snakes with a variety of color patterns, including a rosy or salmon-colored underside, spotting of dark orange to pink along the back, and three lines down their back. The color of the stripes varies and can be shades of brown, orange-red, and black. They have vertical pupils and a long, finger-shaped head.

Did you know?

The Gila monster is the largest lizard native to the US. It is a member of the *Helodermatidae* family, the only family of venomous lizards in the world. The Gila monster can eat a third of its body weight in one sitting. There is a medicine that helps manage diabetes that is based on the protein that is found in the saliva (spit) of the Gila monster; the medicine is sometimes called lizard spit.

Most Active   Hibernates

Safety Note: This lizard is venomous (toxic). If you see one, observe or admire it from a distance.

Gila Monster

Heloderma suspectum

Size: 21½ inches long; weighs 1½–3 pounds

Habitat: Deserts, shrubby areas, rocky foothills, hillsides, and mountain slopes

Range: They can be found in the southwestern US, from southeastern California to Nevada, Utah, Arizona, and New Mexico. It is found across most of western and southern Arizona.

Food: They are carnivores that feed on young mammals, nestlings, eggs of birds and reptiles, lizards, and carrion.

Mating: Spring

Nest: Burrows dug in rocky foothills

Eggs: 3–13 leathery eggs are laid. Females usually lay a clutch of eggs every other year.

Young: The 6-inch hatchlings hatch 4 months after incubation. Hatchlings are independent and will reach maturity in 3–5 years.

Predators: They have very few natural predators, including hawks, owls, coyotes, humans, and snakes.

Gila monsters are venomous, thick-bodied lizards with special bead-like scales. They are black with orange, yellow, or pinkish blotches on their back and irregular lines on their tail. They have a smooth belly. Their venom glands are in their lower jaw and are mainly used for defense from a predator, not as a tool for hunting. They are either diurnal or nocturnal, depending on the temperature.

Did you know?

Females can produce over 45,000 eggs, but the average is usually around 10,000. The temperature can affect the rate that Great Plains toads go through metamorphosis; if the temperature is too warm and the water that they are living in is in risk of drying out, they undergo the process faster. The males let out a long, loud trill during the breeding season to attract mates.

Most Active   Hibernates

Great Plains Toad

Anaxyrus cognatus

Size: 2–3½ inches long; weighs 2 ounces

Habitat: Plains, grasslands, sandhills, farm areas, and semi-desert shrublands

Range: They are found in portions of southern Canada and several states of the Midwest and southwestern United States. They are common across the state of Arizona.

Food: Worms, beetles, ants, and other insects

Mating: Breeds mainly in late spring and early summer, in pools, ponds, and reservoirs

Nest: No nest is built; females use shallow bodies of water (no more than 12 inches deep) to lay eggs in.

Eggs: Females lay around 11,000 eggs at one time. Eggs are laid in a row of long strings that are nestled in two layers of jelly. Females can lay over 20,000 eggs in one season.

Young: Tadpoles hatch 2–7 days after being laid. Tadpoles metamorphose or change into small toads in about 2 months. They reach maturity within 3–5 years.

Predators: Raccoons, water bugs, fish, hognose snakes, grackles, and skunks

Great Plains toads can be identified by their round snout, dry warty skin, and large eyes that sit on the top of their head. They have two ridges or crests above each eye that combine and make a bump on their snout called a "boss." They come in various colors of creams to tans, with blotches of darker tans, browns, and greens covering their body. They have a large parotid gland behind each eye. Their underside is light brown to cream with no spots.

Did you know?

Spadefoot toads get their name from the spade-like projection that is on each hind foot. Males will call while floating around ponds, and they can eat as much as 50% of their body weight in a single night. Like other toads, Mexican spadefoot toads will emit a toxic secretion from the parotid gland when captured by a predator or human. This secretion has a slight peanut butter aroma to it.

Most Active   Hibernates

Mexican Spadefoot Toad

Spea multiplicata

Size: 1½–2½ inches long; weighs 1¾–3½ ounces

Habitat: Wetlands, deserts, freshwater areas, desert scrublands, grasslands, and woodlands

Range: They are found from Utah southward into Colorado, Oklahoma, Texas, Arizona, and Mexico. They are found across most of eastern and central Arizona.

Food: They are carnivores that eat insects and spiders; as tadpoles, they eat algae and fairy shrimp.

Mating: Summer, during monsoon season

Nest: No nest; eggs are laid in water attached to vegetation.

Eggs: Eggs are laid in large masses of 1,000 or more in a single night.

Young: Eggs hatch in 2–3 days and are independent as tadpoles. Most tadpoles go through metamorphosis in 12–19 days.

Predators: Owls, herons, snakes, coyotes, and fish

The Mexican spadefoot toad is a large brown, grayish-brown, or dusky-olive-brown frog (not toad, despite its name) with dark spots, many of which are red tipped. They have large eyes and a wedge- or spade-shaped projection on each of their hind legs that helps to dig into soil. They spend most of the year underground and usually come out during the breeding season.

Did you know?
Leopard frogs are used by humans in many ways, including in research for medical projects and as specimens for biology courses. During the winter, they will hibernate underwater in ponds that have lots of oxygen and do not freeze.

Most Active Hibernates

Northern Leopard Frog

Lithobates pipiens

Size: 2½–4½ inches long; weighs ½–3 ounces

Habitat: Meadows, open fields, lakes, forest edges, and ponds

Range: In Arizona, they are found statewide; there are strong populations into Canada and throughout the northeastern states, with populations extending into northern California, the Pacific Northwest, and the Southwest.

Food: Spiders, worms, insects, and other invertebrates like crustaceans and mollusks

Mating: Late March to early June; mating occurs in water.

Nest: No nest is constructed; within 3 days of mating, the female will lay eggs in permanent shallow bodies of water, attached to vegetation just below the surface.

Eggs: A few hundred to 7,000 or more eggs are laid in one egg mass that is 2–5 inches wide.

Young: Tadpoles hatch about 2–3 weeks after eggs are laid and then complete the metamorphic cycle to become frogs in around 3 months. They reach reproductive maturity in the first or second year for males and within 2–3 years for females.

Predators: Fish, frogs, herons, snakes, hawks, turtles, and dragonfly larvae

The northern leopard frog is a smooth-skinned frog with 2–3 rows of dark spots with a lighter outline around them, atop a brown or green base layer. It has a ridge that extends from the base of the eye to the rear of the frog. They have a white underside. Juveniles (young) will use streams and drainage ditches with vegetation to reach seasonal habitats.

Did you know?

While ornate box turtles are mainly land dwellers, they are able to float and swim decently due to fat deposits under their shells. During the winter, they bury themselves in sandy soil to avoid freezing.

Most Active   Hibernates

Ornate Box Turtle

Terrapene ornata

Size: 4½–5 inches long; weighs ½–1½ pounds

Habitat: Forests, open grasslands, pastures, shrublands, wetlands, farm fields, and marsh meadows

Range: Can be found as far north as Wisconsin, as far east as Louisiana, as far west as Arizona, and as far south as Texas into Mexico. They can be found in the eastern corner of Arizona.

Food: Omnivores, they eat earthworms, berries, beetles, grasses and other plants, and carrion (dead animals).

Mating: Late spring–early summer

Nest: Shallow, flask- shaped burrow built in loose material (dirt, soil, sandy clay)

Eggs: 2–8 eggs

Young: Hatchlings hatch 75–90 days after eggs are laid and will reach reproductive maturity at around 5 years for males and 8 years for females.

Predators: Crows, ravens, hawks, owls, raccoons, cats, foxes, and snakes

Ornate box turtles have sharp beaks, thick limbs, and a flattened dome-shaped carapace (top of shell). The carapace is brownish to black and has a starburst-like pattern on it. The skin is grayish brown with orange-to-yellow spots. They have a yellow or pale-greenish chin. Males have red-hued legs and a large inner claw. Males also have reddish eyes, while females have brown. Males are usually smaller than females.

Did you know?

Red-spotted toads are wrestlers! During the breeding season, males will wrestle to defend their territory. They are the only toads in America that lay eggs individually. Red-spotted toads can lose around 40% of the water in their body and continue to be active.

Most Active   Hibernates

Red-spotted Toad

Anaxyrus punctatus

Size: 3 inches long; weighs less than ½ ounce

Habitat: Rocky canyons, near streams, grasslands, and forests

Range: They can be found in southwestern North America in Mexico, California, Nevada, Utah, Colorado, and a few other states. They can be found across the state of Arizona.

Food: They are carnivores that eat ants, beetles, and other insects, as well as other amphibians.

Mating: March–June

Nest: No nest; females lay eggs underwater, attached to vegetation.

Eggs: Females lay individual eggs; clutches can have over 4,000 eggs.

Young: After hatching, tadpoles go through metamorphosis to turn into adults in 6–8 weeks.

Predators: Birds, foxes, coyotes, bobcats, snakes, and raccoons

Red-spotted toads are small brown toads with round parotid glands that sit on the head behind each eye. They have red-orange warts along their back. The head is short, triangular, and flattened with a pointed snout.

Did you know?

Sidewinders are the fastest moving of all rattlesnakes! Sidewinders get their name from their sideways movement across sand. Their body moves in an S-shape curve, so they are able to move rapidly without much of their body touching the ground at one time. Many scientists and engineers design robots that resemble the sidewinder's movements. When humans use ideas from nature to design technology, it's called biomimicry.

Most Active   Hibernates

Safety Note: These snakes are venomous (toxic). If you see one, observe or admire it from a distance.

122

Sidewinder Rattlesnake
Crotalus cerastes

Size: 17–33 inches long; weighs 3¼–10½ ounces

Habitat: Deserts, rocky areas, and dunes

Range: They are found in the southwestern United States in southeastern California, southern Nevada, southwestern Utah, and western Arizona, as well as northwestern Mexico.

Food: They are carnivores that eat mice, lizards, snakes, and birds.

Mating: April–May, and sometimes in the fall

Nest: Gives live birth in a burrow

Eggs: No eggs; gives live birth

Young: 5–12 young (snakelets) are born after a 4–5-month pregnancy. They are independent at birth and reach reproductive maturity at around 2–3 years of age.

Predators: Kingsnakes, birds of prey, and coyotes

Sidewinders are small tan, cream, and light-brown snakes. They have an arrow-shaped head with raised scales on top of their eyes. They have a face stripe that extends from the eye to the corner of their mouth and vertical pupils. They have brown or grayish-brown splotches down their back. The black-and-white banding at the base of their tail makes it look like prey. They bury themselves in sand with just the rattle sticking out and wave it back and forth to lure in food. They are nocturnal during the summer and crepuscular during the winter months.

Did you know?

Sonoran Desert toads are the largest toads found in North America. The toxins that they secrete can make humans feel sick and see things that are not there (hallucinate); because of this effect, many states have passed laws against licking this toad. It has smoother skin than other toads, like that of a frog.

Most Active   Hibernates

Sonoran Desert Toad

Incilius alvarius

Size: 4–7 inches long; weighs 10½ ounces

Habitat: Grasslands, ponds, forests, lowlands, canyons, canals, ponds, lakes, woodlands, and deserts

Range: This species occurs across southern Arizona, as well as in California, New Mexico, and Mexico.

Food: They are carnivores that feed on insects, lizards, mice, spiders, centipedes, and other amphibians.

Mating: May–July

Nest: No nest; eggs are laid in water.

Eggs: Females deposit long strings of up to 8,000 eggs in shallow or slow-moving water.

Young: Tadpoles hatch anywhere from 2–12 days and will go through metamorphosis in a month or so. Tadpoles are independent at hatching.

Predators: Snakes, birds of prey, and other amphibians

The Sonoran Desert toad is a large toad that looks similar to a frog due its smooth skin. They are brown or olive green in color. They have a crest on the head and parotoid glands that identify them as toads instead of frogs. Young toads have small dark spots with orange tips on their back. Tadpoles are gray or brown and have a round tail tip. When threatened, the toads will secrete a white toxin from their parotoid glands.

Did you know?

Sonoran Desert tortoises can store water in their bladder! This allows them to go long periods without food and water. Desert tortoises are able to burrow underground to escape the heat; in fact, they spend most of their life in burrows and under rocks to help regulate the temperature of their bodies and prevent water loss.

Most Active   Hibernates

Sonoran Desert Tortoise

Gopherus morafkai

Size: 14 inches long; weighs 8–15 pounds

Habitat: Grasslands, valleys, scrub areas, woodlands, canyons, mountain slopes, and hillsides

Range: In North America, they can be found in the eastern portion of California, Nevada, Utah, Arizona, and Mexico. In Arizona, they are found in the southwestern portion of the state.

Food: They are herbivores that feed on cacti, grasses, wildflowers, tree saplings, and other plants.

Mating: June–August

Nest: Eggs are laid in a burrow.

Eggs: 2–15 eggs are laid.

Young: Hatchlings are 2–2½ inches long when they hatch. They are independent at hatching and reach sexual maturity around 15–20 years.

Predators: Ravens, Gila monsters, foxes, roadrunners, and coyotes

Sonoran Desert tortoises have a large dome-shaped shell with growth rings. They are brownish orange, grayish brown, or dark gray in color. Their underside is dusky yellow or tan. They have short tails and thick, short limbs. Their front limbs are less round than the back limbs to aid in digging. All limbs have thick scales. They have a small rounded head, and males have a throat shield.

Did you know?
Like other kingsnakes, the Sonoran mountain kingsnake is immune to rattlesnake venom. They use a type of imitation called Batesian mimicry, where their coloration mimics that of the coral snake (a venomous snake), even though they are nonvenomous.

Most Active   Hibernates

Sonoran Mountain Kingsnake

Lampropeltis pyromelana

Size: 18–43 inches long; weighs 1–3 pounds

Habitat: Rocky slopes, canyon bottoms, mountainous areas, and cliffs

Range: Their range extends from central-eastern Nevada and western Utah southward to Arizona and New Mexico. In Arizona, it can be found from the eastern to western corner along the central area of the state. In the eastern corner, the population has a more spread-out range.

Food: Carnivores, they feed on bats, birds, lizards, and rodents.

Mating: Spring

Nest: Under debris or in rotting logs

Eggs: 3–6 eggs are laid in late spring to early summer.

Young: Young hatch 2–3 months after laying. They are independent at hatching and reach reproductive age at around 3–4 years old.

Predators: Birds of prey, raccoons, skunks, foxes, and bobcats

The Sonoran mountain kingsnake is a medium-size snake that has an alternating pattern of red, black, and white bands. The black bands become broader around the middle of the back and skinnier down the sides. The white bands are surrounded by black bands. They have a white snout, round pupils, and smooth shiny scales.

Did you know?

Horned lizards are named for the crown of horns on their head. Although sometimes called horned toad, horned frog, or horny toad, they are not amphibians, but reptiles. When threatened, horned lizards will inflate themselves with air to look larger. If this technique doesn't work, they can spray blood from the corners of their eyes, confusing predators and allowing them to escape.

Most Active   Hibernates

Texas Horned Lizard

Phrynosoma cornutum

Size: 2½–4 inches long; weighs 1–3½ ounces

Habitat: Plains, grasslands, open dry areas, prairies, and sandy areas

Range: They are found in the south-central United States to northern Mexico. In Arizona, they are found in the southeastern corner of the state.

Food: Harvester ants make up most of their diet, but they will eat other ants and insects, as well as spiders.

Mating: Mid-April to mid-June after hibernation

Nest: Females dig a nest in loose soil or under large rocks.

Eggs: Females lay 14–37 eggs in late May, June, or July.

Young: Eggs hatch within 1–2 months after laying. They are independent at hatching and will reach reproductive maturity at around 2 years.

Predators: Lizards, ground squirrels, hawks, coyotes, snakes, roadrunners, and pet cats and dogs

Texas horned lizards are small but stocky (wide and flat-bodied). Two rows of enlarged fringed scales run down both sides of their body. Their limbs have pointed scales. They have multiple horns on their head, with two of them longer than the others. Most horned lizards have a light-tan or buffy-colored line that extends down their back. They have two large dark spots behind their head, with more dark markings along their back. Their underside is tan to cream-colored.

Did you know?

When threatened, the western banded gecko will freeze and mimic a scorpion by holding its tail above its body and moving it side to side; if that doesn't work, it will detach its tail and run away, leaving the predator to go after its flopping tail. The tail has storage areas for fat and water that can be used when food is scarce.

Most Active   Hibernates

Western Banded Gecko

Coleonyx variegatus

Size: 3 inches long; weighs around 2 grams

Habitat: Dry rocky areas, canyons, grasslands, deserts, and rock piles

Range: This lizard is distributed across most of western and southern Arizona, and they can be found in the southeastern tip of Nevada, central and southeastern California, and western Mexico.

Food: They eat insects, spiders, and other soft-bodied organisms called arthropods.

Mating: April–May

Nest: Females lay eggs under flat rocks.

Eggs: 1–2 smooth, white-shelled, oblong or oval-shaped eggs

Young: Young hatch about 6 weeks after laying. They look like adults and have brown bands that fade into lighter yellow as they age. Young reach reproductive maturity shortly after they hatch.

Predators: Snakes, lizards, and tarantulas

Western banded geckos have light-brown bodies with alternating bands of brown, yellow or cream, and sometimes pink. They are slim with slender legs. Their tail is equal to their body length. They have a triangular head and big eyes with vertical pupils and eyelids. Males have spurs at the base of their tail on both sides.

Did you know?

A rattlesnake will rattle the base of its tail to warn would-be predators; it can move its rattle back and forth 60 or more times a second. Rattlesnakes are venomous (their bites inject toxin), so do not go near one or try to pick one up! Instead, leave it alone so it can help people by munching on rodents and other pests. Rattlesnakes are "pit vipers," snakes that have a special body part that helps them "see" heat.

Most Active   Hibernates

Safety Note: These snakes are venomous (toxic). If you see one, observe or admire it from a distance.

134

Western Diamondback Rattlesnake

Crotalus atrox

Size: 3–5 feet long; weighs 3–14 pounds

Habitat: Rocky hillside, grassy plains, coastal areas, deserts, and forests

Range: They are found in the southwestern states of the US from California to Texas and the northern half of Mexico. In Arizona, they are found in most of the state from the central-western border southward to the Mexico border and eastward to New Mexico.

Food: Carnivores, they feed on mice, rats, rabbits, gophers, ground-dwelling birds, and lizards.

Mating: Spring following hibernation

Nest: Gives live birth in a burrow or hollow log

Eggs: No eggs; young are birthed live.

Young: 10–12 young are born at a time. Young will stay with the mother for a few hours and scatter to find shelter and live independently. Young have fangs and venom at birth. They reach reproductive maturity at around 3 years.

Predators: Coyotes, eagles, hawks, foxes, kingsnakes, bobcats, and roadrunners

The western diamondback rattlesnake is a thick snake with an arrow- or triangle-shaped head. Two diagonal lines that are dark colored run from the mouth to the eyes, as if it is wearing a mask. It has dark, diamond-shaped patterns that run down its olive-brown or tan body. The diamond pattern on its back is where it gets its name.

Did you know?

The western tiger salamander can grow up to 14 inches long and and live over 20 years! Western tiger salamanders migrate to their birthplace to breed. Tiger salamanders have a hidden weapon! They produce a poisonous toxin that is secreted or released from two glands in their tail. This toxin makes them taste bad to predators and allows them to escape.

Most Active   Hibernates

Western Tiger Salamander

Ambystoma mavortium

Size: 7–14 inches long; weighs 4½ ounces

Habitat: Woodlands, marshes, and meadows; they spend most of their time underground in burrows.

Range: In Arizona, they are found almost statewide; populations are found in the western United States.

Food: They are carnivores that eat insects, frogs, worms, and snails.

Mating: Tiger salamanders leave their burrows to find standing bodies of freshwater. They breed in late winter and early spring after the ground has thawed.

Nest: No nest, but eggs are joined together into one group in a jelly-like sack called an egg mass. An egg mass is attached to grass, leaves, and other plant material at the bottom of a pond.

Eggs: There are 20–100 eggs or more in an egg mass.

Young: Eggs hatch after 2 weeks, and the young are fully aquatic with external gills. Limbs develop shortly after hatching; within 3 months, the young are fully grown but will hang around in a vernal pool. Individuals living in permanent ponds can take up to 6 months to fully develop.

Predators: Young are preyed upon by diving beetles, fish, turtles, and herons. Adults are preyed upon by snakes, owls, and badgers.

Western tiger salamanders have thick black, brown, or grayish bodies with uneven spots of yellow, tan, brown, or green along the head and body. The underside is usually a variation of yellow. Males are usually larger and thicker than females.

Glossary

Adaptation—An animal's physical (outward) or behavioral (inward) adjustment to changes in the environment.

Amphibian—A small animal with a backbone, has moist skin, and lacks scales. Most amphibians start out as an egg, live at least part of their life in water, and finish life as a land dweller.

Biome—A part or region of Earth that has a particular type of climate and animals and plants that adapted to live in the area.

Bird—A group of animals that all have two legs and feet, a beak, feathers, and wings; while not all birds fly, all birds lay eggs.

Brood—A group of young birds that hatch at the same time and with the same mother.

Carnivore—An animal that primarily eats other animals.

Clutch—The number of eggs an animal lays during one nesting period; an animal can lay more than one clutch each season.

Crepuscular—The hours before sunset or just after sunrise; some animals have adapted to be most active during these low-light times.

Diurnal—During the day; many animals are most active during the daytime.

Ecosystem—A group of animals and plants that interact with each other and the physical area that they live in.

Evolution—A process of change in a species or a group of animals that are all the same kind; evolution happens over several generations or in a group of animals living around the same time; evolution happens through adaptation, or physical and biological changes to better fit the environment over time.

Fledgling—A baby bird that has developed flight feathers and has left the nest.

Gestation—The length of time a developing animal is carried in its mother's womb.

Herbivore—An animal that primarily eats plants.

Hibernate—A survival strategy or process where animals "slow down" and go into a long period of reduced activity to survive winter or seasonal changes; during hibernation, activities like feeding, breathing, and converting food to energy all stop.

Insectivore—An animal whose diet consists of insects.

Incubate—When a bird warms eggs by sitting on them.

Invasive—A nonnative animal that outcompetes native animals in a particular area, harming the environment.

Mammal—An air-breathing, warm-blooded, fur- or hair-covered animal with a backbone. All mammals produce milk and usually give birth to live young.

Migration—When animals move from one area to another. Migration usually occurs seasonally, but it can also happen due to biological processes, such as breeding.

Molt—When animals shed or drop their skin, feathers, or shell.

Nocturnal—At night; many animals are most active at night.

Piscivore—An animal that eats mainly fish.

Predator—An animal that hunts (and eats) other animals.

Raptor—A group of birds that all have a curved beak and sharp talons; they hunt or feed on other animals. Also known as a bird of prey.

Reptile—An egg-laying, air-breathing, cold-blooded animal that has a backbone and skin made of scales, which crawls on its belly or uses stubby legs to get around.

Scat—The waste product that animals release from their bodies; another word for it is poop or droppings.

Talon—The claw on the feet seen on raptors and birds of prey.

Torpor—A form of hibernation in which an animal slows down its breathing and heart rate; torpor ranges from a few hours at a time to a whole day. Torpor does not involve a deep sleep.

Checklist

☐ American Badger

☐ American Hog-nosed Skunk

☐ Arizona Myotis

☐ Bighorn Sheep

☐ Black Bear

☐ Black-footed Ferret

☐ Black-tailed Jackrabbit

☐ Black-tailed Prairie Dog

☐ Bobcat

☐ Collared Peccary

☐ Coyote

☐ Desert Shrew

☐ Elk

☐ Merriam's Kangaroo Rat

☐ Mexican Free-tailed Bat

☐ Mexican Gray Wolf

☐ Mountain Lion

☐ Mule Deer

☐ Northern Raccoon

☐ Pronghorn

☐ Ringtail

☐ Striped Skunk

☐ White-nosed Coati

☐ American Kestrel

☐ Bald Eagle

☐ Burrowing Owl

☐ Cactus Wren

☐ Elf Owl

☐ Gila Woodpecker

☐ Golden Eagle

☐ Great Blue Heron

☐ Great Horned Owl

☐ Great-tailed Grackle

☐ Greater Roadrunner

☐ Hairy/Downy Woodpecker

☐ Harris's Hawk

☐ Northern Cardinal

☐ Osprey

☐ Peregrine Falcon

☐ Phainopepla

☐ Red-tailed Hawk

☐ Red-winged Blackbird

☐ Say's Phoebe

☐ Wild Turkey

☐ Wood Duck

Reptiles and Amphibians

- ☐ Arizona Tree Frog
- ☐ Chihuahuan Nightsnake
- ☐ Desert Iguana
- ☐ Desert Rosy Boa
- ☐ Gila Monster
- ☐ Great Plains Toad
- ☐ Mexican Spadefoot Toad
- ☐ Northern Leopard Frog
- ☐ Ornate Box Turtle
- ☐ Red-spotted Toad
- ☐ Sidewinder Rattlesnake
- ☐ Sonoran Desert Toad
- ☐ Sonoran Desert Tortoise
- ☐ Sonoran Mountain Kingsnake
- ☐ Texas Horned Lizard
- ☐ Western Banded Gecko
- ☐ Western Diamondback Rattlesnake
- ☐ Western Tiger Salamander

The Art of Conservation®

Featuring two signature programs, The Songbird Art Contest™ and The Fish Art Contest®, the Art of Conservation programs celebrate the arts as a cornerstone to conservation. To enter, youth artists create an original hand-drawn illustration and written essay, story, or poem synthesizing what they have learned. The contests are FREE to enter and open to students in K-12. For program updates, rules, guidelines, and entry forms, visit: www.TheArtofConservation.org

The Fish Art Contest® introduces youth to the wonders of fish, the joy of fishing, and the importance of aquatic conservation. The Fish Art Contest uses art, science, and creative writing to foster connections to the outdoors and inspire the next generation of stewards. Participants are encouraged to use the Fish On! lesson plan, then submit an original, handmade piece of artwork to compete for prizes and international recognition.

The Songbird Art Contest® explores the wonders and species diversity of North American songbirds. Raising awareness and educating the public on bird conservation, the Songbird program builds stewardship, encourages outdoors participation, and promotes the discovery of nature.

Photo Credits

About the Author

Alex Troutman is a wildlife biologist, birder, nature enthusiast, and science communicator from Austell, Georgia. He has a passion for sharing the wonders of nature and introducing the younger generation to the outdoors. He holds both a bachelor's degree and a master's degree in biology from Georgia Southern University (the Real GSU), with a focus in conservation.

Because he knows what it feels like to not see individuals who look like you (or come from a similar background) doing the things you enjoy or working in the career that you aspire to be in, Alex makes a point not only to be that representation for the younger generation, but also to make sure that kids have exposure to the careers they are interested in and the diverse scientists working in those careers.

Alex is the co-organizer of several Black in X weeks, including Black Birders Week, Black Mammologists Week, and Black in Marine Science Week. This movement encourages diversity in nature, the celebration of Black individual scientists, awareness of Black nature enthusiasts, and diversity in STEAM fields.

ABOUT ADVENTUREKEEN

We are an independent nature and outdoor activity publisher. Our founding dates back more than 40 years, guided then and now by our love of being in the woods and on the water, by our passion for reading and books, and by the sense of wonder and discovery made possible by spending time recreating outdoors in beautiful places. It is our mission to share that wonder and fun with our readers, especially with those who haven't yet experienced all the physical and mental health benefits that nature and outdoor activity can bring. #bewellbeoutdoors